Artificial Light /
A Narrative Inquiry into the
Nature of Abstraction, Immediacy, and
other Architectural Fictions

/

The notion of immediacy is not immediate.

Sensory experience does not underlay culture; it is a product of it.

There are as many things as there are views of things.

Artificial Light /
A Narrative Inquiry into the
Nature of Abstraction, Immediacy, and
other Architectural Fictions / *Keith Mitnick* /
Princeton Architectural Press / New York

Published by
Princeton Architectural Press
37 East Seventh Street
New York, New York 10003

For a free catalog of books, call 1.800.722.6657.
Visit our website at www.papress.com.

Editors: Nancy Eklund Later and Linda Lee
Designer: Jan Haux

Special thanks to: Nettie Aljian, Sara Bader, Dorothy Ball, Nicola Bednarek, Janet Behning,
Becca Casbon, Penny (Yuen Pik) Chu, Russell Fernandez, Pete Fitzpatrick, Wendy Fuller,
Clare Jacobson, John King, Aileen Kwun, Laurie Manfra, Katharine Myers, Lauren Nelson
Packard, Jennifer Thompson, Arnoud Verhaeghe, Paul Wagner, Joseph Weston, and Deb Wood
of Princeton Architectural Press —Kevin C. Lippert, publisher

Library of Congress Cataloging-in-Publication Data
Mitnick, Keith.
Artificial light : a narrative inquiry into the nature of abstraction, immediacy, and other
architectural fictions / Keith Mitnick.
p. cm.
ISBN 978-1-56898-749-1 (pbk. : alk. paper)
1. Architecture—Philosophy. I. Title.
NA2500.M58 2008
720.1—dc22
                                                                    2007042492

To Mireille

Contents /

Preface /

This book is the result of a recent trip to the Jersey Shore, where I used to spend my summers as a child. It was the first time I had been back in many years, and the experience brought back vivid memories. While I was there, I began taking photographs and writing about the various places I remembered from childhood. I eventually became obsessed by the very same rollercoaster that had both attracted and terrified me as a kid and spent hours watching its appearance change throughout the course of many days.

I traveled back to the Jersey Shore several more times that summer to take pictures and revel in the lights of the Ferris wheels, the rollercoaster, and the smells and sounds of the boardwalk. At times it felt as though I were looking at the original source of my desire for architecture, and at others a useful context for contemplating concepts that couldn't have possibly been on the minds of those who built it. This book attempts to make sense of those disparate impressions.

Acknowledgments /

First and foremost I would like to thank my friends and collaborators Mireille Roddier and Stewart Hicks. Without them, there wouldn't be much to go on. A lot of people have helped with this book by discussing its ideas and providing encouragement. Among them are Vincent Castagnacci, Caroline Constant, Andrew Herscher, Gillian White, James Woolard, and Claire Zimmerman. Joshua Clover and Robert Levit have inspired me in ways that are difficult to define. I also owe a lot to my family, the members of which are implicated in much of the book's content. I trust they will read it in good humor. I am especially grateful to Princeton Architectural Press for plucking my manuscript from their unsolicited mail and seeing a book in it.

Introduction /

This project looks at the concept of *immediacy*, including the related themes of *affect, abstraction, fakeness,* and *authenticity*, from multiple viewpoints in order to broaden the field in which such themes may be contemplated. The aim throughout is to present unusual readings of familiar terms that challenge the authority of the formal styles and discursive canons that have, paradoxically, come to signify direct experience.

The notion that interpretation gets in the way of our experience of things is an odd, yet recurring, one expressed in many discussions of architecture. It presumes that we could perceive things without, in one way or another, trying to make sense of them and that objects have characteristics independent of our perception of them. Nevertheless the idea of immediacy remains popular among those who would have us stop thinking so much and just let things be as they are, as if to imply that everything occurs directly, without our participation, according to some underlying natural pattern.

But ideology always tries to disguise itself as the outcome of natural and pragmatic forces, and it uses architecture to stage the deception. Given that there are many opposing beliefs vying for naturalness at the same time, we are invariably confronted by the need for multiple natures, which presents a problem, because nature needs to be defined as a single, all-encompassing entity or else it ceases to play the role that ideology requires of it. Nevertheless our experience of the world is rife with gaps between competing belief systems and their presumed correspondence to, or identification with, the different ways that sensory experience is constructed and represented.

In many discussions about architecture, sensation is assumed to be direct, and therefore more real than interpretation. Recent critical (or so-called post-critical) trends have called for a refocusing upon architecture's role as a producer of affects, both as a source of its directness and as a means of discursively screening-out other factors—social, political, economic—that have traditionally defined the discipline. On one hand is an argument about the nature of sensory factors in the creation of "meaningful" experiences and on the other is a desire to shift architectural dialogue and production away from a perceived preoccupation with meaning.

As is the case with all forms of visual culture, the medium is, to a large extent, the message. The way we experience the world is the result of how we represent it. Our terms and standards for normalcy and eccentricity, complicity and deviance, are each determined by the very instruments with which they are recorded and the resulting documents through which they are presented and made sense of.

Recently, new types of media, including reality television and YouTube, have put customary notions of what is real, and what is not, into question by framing the construction of "realness" as part of the very reality they produce. This book contributes to these ongoing debates and creative trends by employing a variety of uncharacteristic methods of description and analysis, including personal anecdotes, allegories, stories, and photographs. Rather than polarizing the contemplation of form between the abstract and the personal, they have been woven together to create an atmosphere in which their interdependence may be understood in new ways. It takes the discussion of architecture in directions that are both particular to its unique position within the visual arts and sympathetic to emergent critical trends in other areas of visual culture. It playfully challenges the presumed correspondence among different types and terms of experience, and the false sense that certain architectural ideas, forms, and representations may be implicitly synonymous.

01

Two-Faced

The other day I went…

...into a health food store to buy a smoothie. The outside was painted in bright tropical colors, and inside there were signs everywhere that said: "Eat Right/Feel Good/Be Happy." Behind the counter was an overweight and unhealthy looking man with smoothie stains running down his shirt, on which was printed the words: "Take Good Care of Yourself." The disparity between his appearance and the spirit of healthiness communicated by the store's décor seemed to disturb a few of the customers. Others savored the contradiction and lingered around to sip their smoothies, as though the charged atmosphere enhanced the flavor of their drinks.

What if architecture did something similar: debunked the very idealizations it stands for at the same time it is standing for them? I imagine a building like the *Titanic*: the most unsinkable of ships sunken upon its maiden voyage, performing its own ideological suicide by advertising its failures rather than the dreams it is presumed to fulfill. Instead of appearing solid and resolute, it would look like a movie set for the staging of multiple realities, and demonstrate conflict and paradox to be the hardcore of architecture rather than the contrivance of order and cohesion we customarily expect from it.

Buildings are like actors that assume different roles, although we tend to regard them as if they possess essential features that define them independently of the circumstances in which they exist. But instead of perpetuating the usual notions about what is real and what is not, what if architecture did the opposite by making things look purposefully fake? Like a magician's handbook, divulging how tricks are made to appear magic, fake architecture could show how ever-changing values and attitudes are dressed up in the costumes of *authenticity, coherence,* and *nature.*

Architecture determines our sense of reality by making concepts look real, and because we tend to believe our senses to be direct, objective, and free of cultural factors, we mistake them for natural phenomena. But architecture is two-faced. It has come to operate across conflicting models of thought and sensation: it is both a shaper of experiences and a sign of them. It teeters between dual roles performed simultaneously to create the illusion that our experience of things agrees with our conceptions of them when the terms of each are mutually exclusive with one another.

We seem to understand phenomenal experience in two different and polarized ways, rather than as a single dynamic in which one set of preconceptions is continually adjusted and reconfigured by the terms of the other. For instance, when we experience the rain falling from the sky, there is the idea of rain, and there is the actual rain. We know that the individual droplets of water are part of a larger body of rainfall, but because the rainfall is beyond our visual comprehension, it has different attributes and associations for us than the raindrops we can touch. It is our relationship to them that makes them mutually exclusive. In a similar way, I know the world does not actually revolve around me, yet I nevertheless stand at the center of all that I perceive. "I" exist as both an abstraction and the nexus of all my experiences.

Objects appear to shrink in size as we move away from them, yet our minds tell us that they remain the same. We believe that what appears to be happening is not actually

happening, yet we typically define reality according to our experience of things rather than our conception of them. We have a hard time believing in "reason" when it contradicts visual appearances, so our minds resolve the gap between sensation and cognition with explanations for the discord. Unable to compensate for the authority of the senses, we continue mistaking sensory experiences for cognitive information.

The misalignment of knowledge and experience doesn't end with visual experience. We convert our knowledge and experiences of the world into abstractions, modeling the relationships between things, ideas, and beliefs into seemingly coherent pictures that look real rather than like pictures. We frame things, organize them into different groupings and classifications that we then use to define them. But names and classifications are not things. In architecture we talk about material effects as being abstract, authentic, and even immaterial, but what could that possibly mean when such terms have nothing to do with material properties other than the associations we have forged between them?

Sometimes we equate such abstractions as permanence and timelessness with architecture because buildings tend to last a long time, even though the meanings that are attributed to them are constantly changing. Like parasites that feed off their hosts until forced elsewhere, ideas move from one building to another. Though a building may initially take form in response to a particular set of ambitions and conceptual strategies, it ultimately exists independent of them. But the fact that the meanings we project upon buildings are mutable does not mean that they are neutral or free of ideology.

In the same way that a computer's operating system correlates disparate data into a common set of terms, our perceptions require a single viewpoint, or logic, to make sense of things. As information is translated into a system, it is altered by the logic of the system through which it is processed. Consequently, the products of our belief systems appear to us to be true because they always cohere to the logic of the dominant belief system through which they are formed. Though such orderings may appear to be natural and real, they register reality about as well as the horizon line describes the edge of the universe.

The disparity among different models of reality is what makes us aware that they are models—multiple perspectives that cannot be collected into a single, homogenous view. In the sense that we create the world through our orderings of it, it is difficult to conceive of something simultaneously through the logic of dissimilar orientations. As is the case with spoken languages, where one may be unaware of the impact of a particular speech pattern upon his thinking until he is able to experience the same thought constructed simultaneously in a different language.

Architecture plays a role in the conversion of disparate thoughts and sensory impressions into a coherent system by relating abstract notions to physical forms. It makes emblems of nature, utility, pragmatism, excess, truth, justice, the sublime, the state, the family, goodness, deceit, and even neutrality by naturalizing them into a view of the world that does not appear to be a view. In many ways this is unavoidable, given that our experience of reality is synonymous with beliefs that have been disguised by architecture to appear real and natural.

Despite the fact that we see the meaning of things changing right before our eyes, we nevertheless expect architecture to convey a pre-existing and unchanging reality rather than the provisional staging of one. We want it to be the irreducible structure of physical matter, not an imitation of it. But rather than trying to block the disparity between how we think about things and the way they appear to us, what if architecture embraced the disconnect by allowing things to exist multifariously, with conflicted identities ascribed according to differing sensibilities? It could come clean with the fact that the sense we make out of the world has very little to do with actual objects and material attributes, and everything to do with the way our abstract notions determine our sense and experience of them.

02

Percept / part 1 /

When I was a kid…

…my parents hired an architect to design a summerhouse for our family. I remember him coming to our home to discuss it with my parents while I played beneath them under the dining-room table. I don't remember their voices, but I do recall the sounds of them turning large pages of blueprints overhead and becoming so overwhelmed by the atmosphere of the conversation that I threw up in the middle of their meeting, right on the leg of my father's pants.

My father was angry and embarrassed and had to excuse himself from the table to change his clothes while the architect waited with my mother, who pretended everything was normal. I could tell she was upset, but I knew from experience that she would not react until after the guest had gone. For her, it was important to behave in front of others as though everything were fine, even when it wasn't. The architect just stood there awkwardly, feeling the tension in the room but not wanting to acknowledge it.

When construction finally began on the new house, the builder invited us over for a big dinner at his home to celebrate. His house was a large suburban structure, covered in endless rows of white shiplap siding with fake black shutters on each of the numerous windows. The house seemed like an overgrown version of something meant to be much smaller. The rooms inside were also strangely oversized; even the yard was immense, seeming more like an empty field than a suburban lawn.

I remember looking out of a second-story window and seeing, in the distance, a series of narrow strips of lawn rolled up into wheels at the end of dirt lanes cut into the grass. I

didn't understand what I was seeing: to me, grass was a part of the ground, not a veneer that could be peeled away. Someone told me that they were making "sod" to sell for other people's lawns. I was perplexed, and I wondered how somebody could sell a lawn. A yard didn't seem like a thing to me, and the fact that it was for sale was disturbing.

As the construction of our new house began to take shape, we would visit the site regularly and have picnics on the nearby beach. Everybody seemed happy on these trips. My parents used to call it their dream-house project: they were building their dream. They told us it was a special "upside-down house," which meant that the living room and kitchen would be upstairs, in order to have a view of the ocean, and the bedrooms were downstairs, for privacy. It was strange to me that my parents dream would be upside down, though in retrospect it was a fitting description for a marriage that would end in divorce only a few years after the completion of the house.

During one of our visits, I remember walking through the house and feeling overwhelmed by the appearance of the exposed-stud wall construction. The array of overlapping walls produced a spellbinding effect as one moved through the space. I was confounded by the elusive sense of shifting centers and alignments I saw among the field of studs. At the same time, I was aware of their logic as soon-to-be-solid walls, as though the same studs participated in two dissimilar systems simultaneously within the same space.

Seeing the house constructed made a huge impression on me as a child: it not only changed my conception of what houses were but also challenged the way I thought about everything. I had mistaken walls to be solid masses of "white stuff," and I thought there was a "right" way to arrange a series of rooms. Like so many other things, I had confused my uninformed assumptions about even the most familiar things for how they actually were. It startled me how easily misled I was and how little I really knew about anything.

I became increasingly obsessed with a belief that there was a fundamental "order" or organization to the world that was not readily apparent—at least not visually—and required effort to comprehend. I looked to things like buildings for clues about what was real and what was not. I used to imagine that I had a little machine that would tell me what was true and what was false. I would ask it questions, and it would give me objective responses. Its only limitation was that it could only deal with "yes" and "no" answers.

Rather than rejecting the rigid black-and-white reductions of my truth-finding device, I only asked questions that could be answered "true" or "false." Sometimes I would project the functions of the truth-finding device to other things, like my elementary school building, asking questions of it as if it were an information machine. I expected tangible objects like buildings to reveal objective premises about the world to me. Not just about material things, like structure and construction, but about deeply personal and emotionally traumatic things. I asked buildings why my parents were breaking up, who I was, and if I would ever be happy: "Yes or no?"

I went to an alternative elementary school founded upon a philosophy of education called "open school." Open school meant that we didn't have individual classrooms but moved throughout various learning areas. The odd thing about it wasn't the openness of the learning format but the ambiguity between the spaces: the ridiculously wide hallways and the wall-to-wall carpet that ran all the way up the walls. Accustomed as I was to a clear distinction among these things—walls and floors, hallways and rooms—I felt uneasy about the blurry boundaries. I worried that I couldn't be certain of things and my relationship to them if the building didn't describe them to me in definitive terms.

In some ways I think that I related to architecture through my anxiety about being deceived. I needed facts to feel secure,

...

and I knew I couldn't always trust the appearance of things. I remember having to go to the bathroom one day in kindergarten, knowing that I needed the boys' room and not the girls' room, but wondering how this had been decided. It seemed to me that the building had enacted this distinction upon me rather than accommodating something I already was.

While we were building our upside-down house, my family was falling apart. I acted as though everything were fine; when my parents would fight, which was often, I pretended it wasn't happening. I wasn't very good at it though, because I believed that if things were going to feel wrong, then they should look that way as well. The actual break-up of my parents was more manageable to me than the deception and denial that preceded it. I could handle the pain and uncertainty that would accompany their inevitable divorce, but I had difficulty pretending everything was fine when it wasn't.

There was a gaping disconnection between appearances and reality in my family. My mother would always put on a happy face if someone stopped by, or force an upbeat voice when she answered the phone, even if she had just been yelling at us, or fighting with my father, or crying. This confused me because I thought it was dishonest: these same people (my parents) had taught me that it was wrong to lie, even though both of them did so repeatedly. My father would say things that were untrue and my mother would perform untruths. Their contradictions and inconsistencies frightened me.

For better or worse, incongruent appearances have fascinated me ever since. A friend told me that when she was a child her mother used to smoke in front of her while simultaneously denying that she was doing so because she didn't want them to think that it was okay to smoke. She would sit in the living room puffing away, and if one of the children entered the room she would put her arm with the cigarette behind the chair, out of view. Sitting there with a smile, smoke rising up in the air behind her, she would pretend there was no cigarette.

In a sense our summerhouse was all smoke and mirrors, even though it represented my parents' dreams of happiness. Buildings lie by staging deceptions about everything from their materiality, their age and manner of construction, to the ideological messages that they embody. They are like television sitcoms about absurdly idealized families: everybody knows it is just an act, a pretense, but somehow we are still seduced by the images of perfection it presents.

Percept / part 2 /

It is the relationship among things—rather than the things themselves—that gives objects their identities. Though we tend to regard them as having stable and enduring characteristics, the determination of "thingness" is more a matter of groupings and classifications than it is a consequence of inherent material properties. Objects require limits in order to be distinguished from the field of reciprocal relations in which they exist, but the limits we impose upon them are a function of our perception rather than a property of their thingness.

Like a collection of books organized into a library or a set of maps configured into an atlas, groupings of subsidiary

parts into larger wholes occur at different scales to produce different identities from the same material. In the case of buildings, a wall may be defined as a coplanar assortment of studs, sheetrock, screws, paint, windows, and doors, but each of these subcomponents in turn comprises another set of secondary elements. The door may be composed of a frame, laminate, panels, knobs, hinges, and locking mechanisms, and the sheetrock out of paper, gypsum, glue, and so on.

Because physical matter may be conceptually broken apart or compounded to yield an infinite array of classifications, the notions by which we separate fields of relationships into parts and wholes are essentially indeterminate. We may define the same arrangement of elements according to multiple and even contradictory orderings that consequently ascribe different properties to the same material: the same elements are understood to be different things at the same time. A wall may be defined by the texture of its surface, its structural properties, or according to the spaces it defines. It may be the vertical continuation of a wrapping floor, the inner lining of a massive facade, or the consequence of a system of formal processes intended to eradicate the very notions of floors, walls, and ceilings.

We understand the world according to our organization of it. Through images, diagrams, language, and other translations, our perception of the physical world is molded according to our representations of it. Therefore, things may only appear to us according to the logic of these abstractions. Our models are provisional, approximate descriptions that extract and isolate an infinitely complex network of relationships in order for them to be intelligible to us. We give the abstractions names, then project the logic of these abstract orderings back upon our perceptions of the world, looking for things according to their names and mistaking recognizable patterns for essential properties.

When my parents eventually broke up, and the family shifted from a group of five to four, we all felt like different people. We stopped doing things together and retreated into our individual worlds. In retrospect it was my father alone who achieved a new life, with another wife and new children—an identity without us. He moved far away to a different climate and became a different person while we stayed behind—the same family minus a father.

03

Affect

When the summerhouse…

...was finally finished, we would go there on weekends and sometimes for the entire summer. For me, the highlight of the season was our visit to the boardwalk in Sea Bright, a few towns to the south. The Sea Bright boardwalk stretched for several miles along the water's edge and was composed of amusement piers, restaurants, stores, and gaming parlors. There was a lot to do and see, but the biggest attraction was simply the hordes of people walking the elevated wooden boardwalk that ran alongside the vast expanse of beach.

It was all bright lights, loud music, and amusements: waterfalls, log flumes, roller coasters, and a huge Ferris wheel. There was pizza, cotton candy, and soft ice cream as well as an endless array of custom t-shirts, cheap jewelry, pot-smoking paraphernalia, and other disposable junk. Though at first glance it may have appeared to be a frenzy of consumption, the excitement of the place had much more to do with the energy and density of the people than anything one might eat or buy. Everybody looked happy, healthy, and on vacation. I couldn't get enough of it.

The people were different from those in our conservative and introverted beach town. They were loud, in-your-face, and full of life. I saw people of every age, ethnicity, and cultural stereotype, from grandparents to little babies and mobs of teenagers. The boardwalk boomed with loud music, screams from amusement riders, the bells and buzzers of arcades, and the voices of competing gamesters trying to lure people to their booths, where they could win overstuffed animals and water pistols.

The later it was, the more the place filled up. The music got louder; the people grew rowdier. There were fistfights, and

I would see teenagers throwing up on the nearby beach from too much beer. Underneath the boardwalk people built fires, made out, and got wasted. For a little kid like me, bored with my normal surroundings and suspicious of my parents' idea of an upside-down dream house, it was absolutely fabulous. I loved all of it: the danger of the rides, the density of bodies, and the general sensory overload. I never wanted to leave the spectacle of sounds and artificial light.

The only problem was my parents despised the place. I had to beg them for weeks beforehand to even think about taking me there. They would promise and promise, but they never wanted to go. Eventually they would give in and commit to an evening. I would go crazy with anticipation, working myself up into an unbearable frenzy of excitement. On the drive there, my father would try to dampen the fun by putting the board-walk down. He thought it was sleazy, but I didn't care what he thought.

As soon as we arrived, he would announce the amount of time that we could stay, the number of rides I could go on, and the amount of junk food I could eat: one slice of pizza, one ice cream, one big lemon freeze, etc. He tried to kill it for me, but my ardor for the place wouldn't die. On the boardwalk I felt alive, lit up like a fireworks display; freed from the perpetual restraint that was always expected of me.

I remember going into the haunted-house attraction alone. At first I was nervous, then terrified. The place wasn't so much "haunted" as it was disorienting. It was a funhouse with fluorescent shapes and abstract objects intended to throw off one's sense of scale and direction. It worked perfectly on me;

after only a few minutes I was so panicked I couldn't think or see straight. I was a hysterical little kid, completely alone in an eerie psychedelic maze.

Eventually, I was able to discern a glowing red emergency-exit sign, just out of view of the other luminous effects and misdirection. I ran for it and found a black door beneath the sign. I shoved my way through it. As the door opened, I launched into a world suspended between two realities: the formless void of the funhouse with its fluorescent shapes, confusing spaces, and terrifying darkness and a view out through the doorway toward the rear of a set of nondescript boardwalk buildings, dumpsters, parking lots, and the caustic glare of streetlamps.

I saw a couple of people standing around as if they were waiting for something, and then I realized that they were my parents. At first I had no idea what they were doing here in this bizarre netherworld of surreal disconnection: they looked like strangers. Everything felt staged and without a center, as though I was slipping between multiple worlds. I felt like I was standing apart from the things, places, and people that had formed me, as if I were looking at them from the outside.

My father was astonished to see me running toward him from the emergency exit and, after a second or two, berated me for sneaking out early. Nevermind that I had been scared out of my mind—this had been the last item on his to-do list before he could get the hell out of the place he so detested. I tried to calm myself down in the hope that we could stay longer, but the adrenaline rush was so intense that I suddenly puked up funnel cakes on his new docksiders. That was all he needed to end my night, and we headed for the car.

As we pulled out of the parking lot, I could see the huge, revolving Ferris wheel looming up over us like a giant celestial motor. It was a simple thing, a big wheel on a stand, but I was mesmerized by its effect. In a single continuous movement it carried people up and down, to and from the sky. The arcing array of light trails produced by the large circle seemed to hang still in the air while the giant wheel spun. All at once I could see and hear people screaming, music blaring, and the spectral of emanating colors pumped out by the circulating pulse of this spinning engine. How a thing could be so beautiful was beyond my comprehension.

Back in the car, with the boardwalk receding in the distance, my ecstasy turned into carsickness as we accelerated onto the New Jersey Turnpike. I watched the road coming toward us through the windshield and saw it receding simultaneously in the rearview mirror. I focused on the intensely yellow lines that divided the lanes of the highway and went into a trance.

My parents complained to one another that they would absolutely never go back to Sea Bright. My sister said it was fine with her because she hated being with us instead of her friends. A big deer lay dead on the edge of the road, and my father swerved to miss it. He cursed while we all slid up against the side of the car. I turned to see the deer out of the rear window, but all I could make out was a lump of thickened darkness, flat and without depth.

04

Abstract / part 1 /

Because all physical things are…

…equally material, the notion that one form of architecture may appear to be more abstract, immaterial, or neutral than another is a consequence of how it is discussed rather than a property of its material features. Abstraction in architecture is frequently associated exclusively with minimal, rectilinear boxlike buildings clad with sleek, homogenous surfaces in which scale and construction are visually diminished. But given that the same collection of materials and effects arranged in an irregular (non-box) shape would appear less minimal, and therefore less neutral, the correspondence of the term *abstraction* with box-buildings is more the result of the recent history of minimalist art and architecture than it is the inherent nature of boxes and smooth surfaces.

Abstraction in architecture is the opposite of what it is in painting, where it signifies the elimination of representation in order to foreground the material effects of surface and texture. In the case of so-called abstract architecture, the objective is to create the illusion of immateriality by eliminating scale and tactility rather than amplifying contrast among them. Nevertheless, the affiliation of such stylized forms with modernist terms of abstraction has led them to infer the kind of nonrepresentational directness associated with the flatness and literalism of non-representational painting.

The reduced-box architectural genre is often cited as free of rhetoric and historical references, able to simply be *itself*—a neutral producer of affects—by virtue of its geometry and materiality. In his book *Supermodernism* (NAi Publishers, 2002), Han Ibeling claims that an architecture that refers "to nothing outside itself and makes no appeal to the intellect"

automatically prioritizes direct experience. But such perspectives fail to account for the fact that these stylizations
are read as markers, held over from a genre of work and ideas
that lay claim to direct, unmediated perception. Abstraction
in architecture has been equated with the blankness, absence,
and purity of monochromatic surfaces and grids appropri-
ated from modern art. It comes with a culturally constructed
presumption of directness that, like the color gray, has come
to represent neutrality rather than enact it.

Abstract / part 2 /

When I was thirteen, my older brother was arrested and sent to prison. Because he was significantly older than me and had left the house when I was very little, I never really knew him. His presence in my life was like that of a shadow. I was acutely aware of his existence but only saw him infrequently—at special events or at strange and unexpected times when something was wrong, like the time he showed up at our house with a sick woman that kept passing out on our front porch until my mother made him take her away for fear of what the neighbors might think.

I knew my brother more from other people's descriptions of him than from any direct personal experience. I constructed an image of him through many, mostly negative, remarks made about him by my parents. For the most part, they avoided talking about him—apparently his life caused them great disappointment—but occasionally a detail would surface that I could add to my collection. In the end I was never sure where my reconstruction ended and where the real person began. Because my mental image of him was so much richer with information than my actual experience, the made-up brother ended up feeling the most real to me.

The fact that my brother was arrested wasn't so surprising, given my image of his life, but he had been accused of murder, and, according to my parents, there was no way he could avoid being convicted for it. I felt numb, though I didn't know it at the time. I wasn't sure how to feel, and it bothered me. I wanted to have clear and definitive emotions about him, but I didn't have much to go on. The idea that he may have murdered somebody scared me. I imagined blood, bullet holes, ambulances, and police chases, though in reality I had no idea what had happened. My parents wouldn't tell me anything, and the void they created around the event made it all the more impossible to make sense of it.

I felt betrayed by the absence of information and vulnerable to my own morbid imagination. It wasn't as though I could choose to leave the matter unresolved in my mind—it needed to take form, to be described and mulled over in order for me to find closure. The vague references presented to me by my parents only confused me further. They created a hole in my mind that stood for him, or more precisely, for what I didn't know about him, and then left it to me to fill it in. But blankness does not remain blank for very long.

The events leading up to my brother's execution were awful. After starving me of information for months, my parents suddenly announced he had been sentenced to death. It struck me as a double negative: how is a blank spot eliminated? Once again, I had no idea how to react to this as the reality of the situation had never been clearly established in the first place. To me he hardly seemed to exist, yet apparently he had requested our presence at the terminal event.

On that last day, we all got in the car to make the three-and-a-half-hour drive to the prison. It was winter; the car was freezing and, as usual, stank of old cigar smoke that made me carsick before we even left the driveway. Everything around looked bleak: gray sky, dirty snow, a melancholic landscape of undifferentiated suburban emptiness. My mother performed normalcy with manic intensity, trying to drown her pain in a

desperately failed imitation that gave the rest of us chills. It was nauseating and surreal, and I kept saying stupid things that I expected to be funny until I heard myself say them. Things like, "Hurry up, he's dying to see us."

By the time we arrived at the front gate of the prison, we were all miserable. The ride had been excruciating, and the sight of the big concrete prison was the first time the ominous feelings brewing inside us became tangible. Everything else merely felt like distant and ambiguous forebodings of death, but the abject banality of this massive concrete box looked like the face of the real thing. As despicable as it was, it gave form to otherwise inchoate suffering.

The inside was even worse. My mother trembled as we moved through the sequence of endless corridors and metal doorways. As we bored deeper into the antiseptic core of the structure, we were increasingly deprived of sensory nourishment. Everything was somber and dark, and there was a stench of bad air delivered in short supply. If we stayed too long, we knew we would quickly use up all of our visual memory from the outside world and be left with only the self-referential array of painted gray concrete and exposed duct systems that surrounded us.

At first I thought the building appeared this way in order to torture its inhabitants. But once we entered the death chamber, I understood things differently. It was completely empty, except for a chair and a white curtain. It resembled a lunar module suspended in deep space, with neither context nor referent. It was a noplace in which odious deeds were presumably contained, absorbed, and ultimately erased. This was a place that not only enacted the terms for so-called surgical executions, but also absolved its perpetuators of their participation in them. I sat there transfixed on the little picture window, wondering if my brother would even appear.

After the event I was approached by one of the prison officials and led to my brother's cell, at the other end of the complex, to collect his things. They told me that he had spent his last days in another area of the building but that his cell was just as he had left it. I felt nauseated by the prospect of being so close to the actual physical details of his former existence, not wanting to give my memory of him any more reality than I could bear, yet compelled by the prospect of knowing him better.

His cell was meticulously clean and well organized, as though nobody lived there. Either the guards had erased all traces of his having been there right after he left, or the space of the cell itself had vanquished his identity long before his final hours. There were lots of books on the shelves and a few photographs perfectly aligned on the wall. I noticed one of the family—me, my parents, grandmother, sister, and cousins on the construction site of the summerhouse—that he must have taken because he was the only one of us not included. I had never seen it before, but it couldn't have been more familiar to me. There we were, comically disfigured like some kind of failed imitation of normalcy. I wondered how this photograph, which was so deeply personal for me, could also have had meaning for a person whom I hardly even knew?

His funeral was a lonely and, with only four of us there, empty affair. An unadorned pine box for a coffin—a symbol I suppose, given my parents' ability to pay for something better, of his supposed moral destitution expressed in the language of financial ruin. A material that would have appeared rustic and precious in other circumstances (a handmade table or toolbox) looked bare-boned and miserable here. They lowered him into the hole, making a terminal void solid, and I said goodbye.

05

Immediate / part 1 /

In many discussions about immediacy…

…in architecture, arguments are made for the ability of architecture to generate perceptual effects that may be experienced without interpretation. But the notion that some effects may be more phenomenological or abstract than others is a peculiar idea, given that all forms are equally material, and such designations signify abstract distinctions rather than physical characteristics.

It is important to clarify the difference between arguments against interpretation and claims made about nature and unmediated experience. On one hand is the call for discursive boundaries to limit how we talk about things; on the other is a claim about how things actually are. The former would include self-referential and formalist arguments as necessary for maintaining disciplinary autonomy, and the latter would include phenomenological discourses in which the certain characteristics of place, building craft, and vernacular forms are understood to be the wellspring of immediacy. One is based on an intellectual idea about the efficacy of critical dialogue, and the other founded upon a belief about the so-called nature of uninterpreted perceptual experience. Although these views may appear to be antithetical, they are both characterized by a theory of "no-theories" that argues against interpretation and for directness.

In some ways the notion of immediacy is the flip-side of abstraction in that immediacy is an abstract concept rather than an attribute of things, and so-called abstract architecture has many of the features associated with the concept of immediacy because it is conceived independently of the particularities of its location and, as a result, frequently gives specific

character to what might otherwise be "placeless" places. To argue for more immediacy in architecture is equivalent to "fighting for peace," where the very formulation contradicts the premise upon which it is founded.

There is a history of the senses that preconditions the way we perceive natural phenomena such as light, shadow, reflection, and color, and these perceptual attributes are no less symbolically rich and mythologized than any human-produced artifact. What could it mean to amplify the sensorial dimensions of architectural experience when all materials and phenomenal effects exist everywhere in equal measure? Would it mean more reflections and subtler lighting or handcrafted details and irregular materials? Such characteristics may be desirable, but they are no more or less immediate than anything else. Immediacy, like any other abstract notions, represents a set of ideological and visual sensibilities cast upon material form.

Immediate / part 2 /

When I was much younger I had a friend named Nick. He was good at everything, and everybody liked him. Nevertheless, he had a strong tendency to disregard the merit of whatever came easily to him—even if it was valued highly by others. Nick used to say that people were attracted to his least attractive features, that is, what they perceived to be his natural abilities and affects. He preferred to identify with what he felt was missing, lost, or underdeveloped about himself rather than his inherent gifts. For Nick talent without strife was automatic and, therefore, meaningless. He used to say that the most popular people must wonder why anybody would like them.

It was never clear to me what my talent was, but being around Nick made it clear what it wasn't. I didn't have endless choices due to exceptional athletic or scholastic abilities, and I certainly wasn't so charismatic that people constantly wanted to be around me. But my friendship with Nick also put into doubt my belief that such characteristics, even though I still wished them for myself, actually brought about the kind of experiences that I perceived to be absent from my own life. Nick's lack of satisfaction with himself was directly linked to his abundant talents, available opportunities, and obvious desirability to others.

Part of Nick's charm was that being with him made you feel good about yourself. For many, his company was like a trophy, a sign of their own desirability, if only by extension. But Nick must have understood this. He must have felt his automatic and innate people-talents performing their customary hypnotic effects even upon his closest friends, putting into question once again the true source of their attraction to him—as though the magnetic force he exerted upon them, what brought them close to him, was in the end what prevented him from ever really feeling close to them.

I first met Nick in the ninth grade, where he showed up one day in the middle of the fall semester. Despite his good looks and the ease with which he made new friends, there was something weird about him. He had, only a week before, been expelled from the military school where he had spent his last three years, and the bizarre social conduct he had acquired from that institution was strangely transposed into our public-school setting. He did odd things like call the teachers "ma'am" or "sir" and turned the hallway corners in crisp and sudden ninety-degree rotations. These affectations would soon fade away, but, as Nick eventually told me, the fear of being suddenly accosted and brutalized by upper classmen did not. He told me that he never really slept soundly or was able to relax—expecting as he always did to be unexpectedly yelled at, trampled, or publicly humiliated (like the time he passed out marching back and forth in formations on a hot summer day wearing a thick wool military uniform, and they made him stand outside in the rain for an entire night as punishment; or when he got caught buying pot with the money his father had sent him to purchase a new saber, and they announced his expulsion on the school-wide intercom).

Despite the tendency of most people to gravitate toward him, Nick failed to ever become identified with any particular clique or social stereotype. I think he would have liked to have been a "burn-out," and smoke pot all day, but he was far too popular to ever win acceptance with such a marginalized group. Besides, even after military school had faded from his persona, he remained oblivious to the subtleties of dress codes and ways of talking required to define him socially. He was a popular loner.

That he and I became best friends is odd. My attraction to him was probably the same as everybody else's, but I never figured out what drew him to me. We never talked about the inequalities between us, though they were glaringly obvious—especially in the company of others. Neither of us had many friends—though he had countless prospects, and I had very few.

One day we realized that Nick's family owned a second house on the bay in the same town where my family had built the summerhouse, and, coincidentally, we ended up spending several summers there at the same time. We spent hours pulling one another up and down Oceanside roads with one of us driving his green moped and the other pulled along on a skateboard with a rope. We went sailing on his Sunfish, played frisbee on the beach, and spent endless hours and quarters at the boardwalk video arcade. With absolutely no effort on our part, we cycled in and out of several orbits of teenage groups whose main pastime seemed to be drinking copious amounts of beer and making out in the sand dunes before puking and passing out. We never lasted long with these groups, but Nick was constantly discovered and pursued by girls who would insist that he spend time with them, and, disinterested as he was in anything but the make-out session, Nick always made me come along.

Though we never talked about it, I knew that Nick was having a hard time with his father. Having met the man myself many times it was easy to see why. He was irritable and over-bearing and constantly told everybody what to do. He adored Nick, compensation for his lousiness as a father it seemed, but he understood absolutely nothing about his son.

Pleased as he was by Nick's superficial successes in school, sports, and with girls, he was also completely oblivious to him. The only times Nick's father ever engaged him in sustained and substantial ways were when Nick did something to piss him off. The more distant and too easily satisfied Nick felt his father to be, the more he tried to anger him. I never knew how conscious this was on Nick's part, but he took the degree of his "acting out" to the next level the summer before our junior year in high school.

I remember him calling me one afternoon and telling me how he had been taking his father's new car out for drives on the nearby Jersey Turnpike at 3:00 a.m. He described how he would quietly roll up the garage door, put the car in neutral, and push it out onto the street so as not to wake anybody up. Nick was about fifteen at the time and had little, if any, driving experience. By the time he lured me into one of his late-night car thefts, he was already comfortable racing the car along the highways at speeds in the upper nineties.

One day he proposed that I come along that night on what would be his longest excursion yet. He wanted to drive forty miles north to Atlantic City, where, according to him, we would drink complimentary casino drinks and gamble into the early morning hours before returning the big new car safely to his father's garage. I should have known then that failure was inevitable—motivated as his actions were by a desire for attention rather than the thrills he purported to crave—but I was too caught up in his enthusiasm to decline what I knew was a stupid undertaking.

I waited up for him until about 2:00 a.m., but when he failed to appear I gave up and went to sleep. An hour or so later, I was awakened by the sight of him crawling through my bedroom window. He had punctured two small holes in the sliding screen windows and pulled the latches in far enough to release the locking mechanism that held them in place. Unable to push them up high enough to create ample crawl space, he went around to the back of our house, opened the small utility shed, and found a stepladder that he carried back around to the front of the house, all in the dark. Not only was he filled with an insatiable need to mess things up for himself, he was also a precocious burglar.

When he crashed down onto the floor of my bedroom, I felt dread at the prospect of what I knew he was about to make me do. I told him it was too late and that I was tired, but he would have nothing of it. We both knew that I wouldn't say no to him. I quickly dressed in the dark, and we quietly slipped out the window onto the stepladder and down the street to where he had parked his father's car. When I got into the car, I was dumbfounded to find his family's tiny pug, Cleo, looking up at me excitedly with her little tongue hanging out. I couldn't tell if she was happy to be a part of delinquency or just terrified. Nick told me she had started barking when he went into the garage and decided to bring her along. Between the front seats of the car, Nick had positioned a newly purchased three-foot-tall plastic bong. I bridled at the abject stupidity of it all

but said nothing. Nick started the car and we headed toward the Atlantic City expressway.

Eventually, we arrived outside of one of the casinos, parked the car, and walked toward the front entrance. It was about 4:00 a.m. by now, and the streets were completely empty. This was hardly the excitement Nick had promised earlier in the day. Unlike Nick, I didn't like getting into trouble. I was growing tired of him and increasingly annoyed by the stupid things he was doing and saying: smoking pot while he drove without a license in a stolen car and bragging about all of the exciting things he was going to do with his life. I wanted to go home, and I told him so. He ignored me, and we continued on to the casino.

Just before we entered the large building, a seedy looking man approached us holding three small cups and a little red ball in his hand. He signaled us over to a nearby stairway, placed the ball on the surface of one of the steps, and covered it with one of the three cups that he placed upside down in a single line. He moved the cups around quickly and asked Nick to guess where the ball was. Predictably, Nick correctly identified the location of the ball three times in a row, was complimented for his abilities by the man, and invited to wager upon his next guess about the location of the ball.

Nick turned to me with a look of assured conspiratorial glee and whispered in my ear that he knew what he was doing and that he wanted to borrow some money for me. He said this was our chance to make a lot of cash, and, if successful, he had lots of ideas about how we could make even more. At that moment I finally admitted to myself how far gone Nick really was and how stupid I had been to listen to him. I turned and walked out of the building and headed toward the car. I didn't know how I would get back to Oceanside, but I had to get away from him.

Nick caught up with me just as I reached his car. Cleo saw us and began jumping up and down hysterically. Nick realized how angry I was and quietly offered to drive us back to Oceanside. We got into the car and, as usual, he over-accelerated and shot the car out into the middle of the road without even looking for oncoming traffic. As we raced toward the highway entrance, it began to rain, a little at first, and then it turned into a downpour. It was still dark outside, and with the rain pouring down, it was increasingly hard to see where we were going. Cleo cowered on my lap and made desperate wheezing noises.

Just when I thought Nick might be calming down and feeling remorse for his recklessness, he turned on the radio and blasted the volume. I wanted to scream. I gripped Cleo tightly until she yelped and tears came to my eyes. Just then the car slid across the flooded surface of the highway, and we began to spin counterclockwise, suddenly crossing over three lanes of the highway. Luckily there were no cars nearby, and we managed to avoid hitting anything until we crashed into a small metal barrier and bounced up and into a grass-covered ditch at the side of the road.

When the car finally stopped moving, we sat there as if hypnotized, unable to comprehend the fact that the car had spun so uncontrollably across the road at high speed without killing us. We looked down, as if expecting to see severed limbs and blood, but everything was okay. Without talking we each got out of the car to appraise the situation. The sun was just beginning to rise, and in the early light I could see that the front and rear axles had been completely crushed. The four wheels were bent outward in an unsettling way, like a human leg bent unnaturally backward. The car was totaled.

Expecting the police to arrive at any moment, I reached inside the car grabbed the bong and threw it as far as I could into the tall grasses that lined the highway. Nick screamed and tried to stop me. I became so totally enraged that I began to scream at him uncontrollably. I had never been comfortable expressing anger before, and the sensation of rage utterly consumed me. I exploded in a way that I had never experienced. The sensation of fear and rage welled up well beyond the limits of my physical body and I felt myself divide into two seemingly concurrent consciousnesses; the first was the angry me and the second a placid observer of the former. I saw Nick terrified by the furor unleashed in me, and despite the fact that I was still yelling at him, I felt profound empathy toward him: I recognized for the first time something of the emotional trauma that precipitated his self-destructiveness.

When the rage subsided, I was a different person. In some ways I felt better than I had in a long time, as though I had unburdened myself of some unknown but unavoidable hardship. I quickly devised a plan of action. I didn't want to wait for the police and deal with what that would involve, so we collected our things from the car, wrote down the mile marker of the crashed car, and set off up the highway with Cleo to find a pay phone. Eventually a car pulled over and offered to drive us most of the way to Oceanside. Sitting in the car, soaking wet and relieved to still be alive, I watched as the morning light intensified and the rain subsided. I knew we were in trouble, but I didn't care so much—everything felt more peaceful to me then it had in a long time, and even Cleo seemed to have calmed down.

We made it back to my house. Everybody was still sleeping. I changed my clothes and got something for Nick to eat. I realized that not only had I survived unscathed but also that nobody in my family would ever find out about what had happened. Nick had no need to tell anyone that I had accompanied him. I felt bad for Nick, knowing how his father would react. I listened as he called and woke up his mom to tell her what had happened. I waited with him until her car appeared at the front of our house. He walked out with Cleo in his arms, got in, and drove off. I didn't hear from him for a long time afterwards.

06

Fake / part 1 /

Prevalent ideas about visual order…

...are being challenged in the visual arts by a growing disinterest in order-making altogether. Surprisingly, the response that most effectively bridges the gap between the ordered and the non-ordered is not the valorization of disorder but the flattening of all elements into a field of uniform significance in which featurelessness itself becomes the primary feature. In the absence of familiar hierarchies and relationships between customary centers and margins, objects take on new relationships to the atmospheres and interstices that they usually stand in front of and, in doing so, appear unreal.

In an attempt to depict this leveling of significance, many photographers explore the relationship of focus to the pictorial structure of their images. In their work conventional experiences of focus and blur as indicators of relative distances are scrambled to allow otherwise peripheral fragments to assume sharp focus while more centrally dominant forms are blurred. In this way the photographs depart from the naturalized version of seeing we have come to expect from photography and present the physical world in new terms that make real things look like diminutive models, or fakes, because they do not adhere to the visual logic to which we are accustomed.

While the specific effects used to create fakeness in photography may not be transferable to architecture, the idea of the contrivance of realness is. Similar to a movie set, where the means of staging an effect or idealization are visible along with the staged performance, architecture stands to challenge its own status as a shaper of reality by ceasing to portray itself as a direct and natural extension of reality. When it appears as a stage set for the creation of an unreal event, the status of the

experience and the meanings conveyed prevaricate and challenge the very basis for the production of realness—a paradoxical circumstance for an art form that by definition has been charged to define and deliver real things.

Sometimes fake things feel more real than the things that they're faking. Because they are reconstructions of something else, they may capture an exaggerated feature of the original that may seem less vivid in its normal context. To put reality into relief, it needs to be overcharged, to be punched out from the environment that it typically extends. It needs to appear like oversaturated color in an otherwise normal color field, like watching a bad actor playing a role in which we notice the acting, without wanting to, because it appears unnatural to its setting.

Fake / part 2 /

My cousin Heather was a precocious teenager. She wasn't particularly intelligent, but she was a genius when it came to sex. She was pretty, self-assured, and liked to party. When she was sixteen, she came to visit my family during our vacation at the summerhouse. The first day Heather came to the beach, every guy within a hundred yards of us took notice. They walked back and forth staring at her idiotically and tossed balls in our direction to give themselves a chance to come closer. Heather was aware of all of this but pretended not to be. She was as obsessed with getting their attention as they were with her, despite her seeming indifference.

In addition to being extremely flirtatious, Heather emanated a mysterious but undeniable magnetism that drove guys nuts, especially the more "manly" among them. The manly type was her primary target: guys who were so sure of themselves that they walked right up to her and asked her out with little or no preamble or small talk. They had big muscles, deep tans, and stylish hair, and were the dumbest sub-breed of humans I had ever met.

When she reached high school, Heather's life started to go wrong. Her parents had divorced and her mom's new drug-dealing boyfriend moved in with them. Heather got heavily into drugs. One day the police knocked on the door of their home with a search warrant. They arrested her mom and the boyfriend—they had a safe full of illegal drugs and cash in the basement—and sent them off to prison. Heather moved in temporarily with her father and his new wife, who despised her. When she turned eighteen, Heather moved to Southern California to become a model. That was the last any of us heard about her for many years.

When I was in college, my sister called to tell me that Heather was appearing in porno movies. At first I didn't believe it; then I felt really bad for her. I pictured her as the victim of some demonic conspiracy against women, manipulated through drug-induced coercion to act against her better judgment. I called my sister to discuss my prognosis and to strategize a family intervention.

After listening briefly to my speculations, my sister interrupted to tell me that I was wrong. She said Heather produced all of her own movies and did mostly lesbian films. She had a line of "signature" products and told her father that she was "finally in control of her own financial future." Dubious, I decided to visit her and see for myself. I made my sister come too.

Heather picked us up at LAX in a black Corvette with the roof down and a license plate that said: "I DARE YOU." When we stopped at traffic lights, guys would pull up beside us and, as usual, stare at her. She had large sunglasses, a super tan, and very little clothing on. The car stereo was blasting, and she was hyper, apparently anxious to show us how successful and in control of her life she was. Despite the no-apologies attitude she affected whenever the subject of pornography came up—

which it did constantly because she kept mentioning it—she seemed unsure, nervous about our perceptions of her.

I faked enthusiasm for her new life and pretended to be comfortable with it all. As usual, the conversation remained entirely focused on her. She talked nonstop about her films, popular misconceptions about the "business," and, in line with our family's core values, what an outrageous amount of money she was making. Back at her oceanfront condo she presented us with her spectacular view, an artificial fireplace with a dimmer switch, and a new line of sex products she was endorsing that included a latex model cast directly from her "unit."

She treated us to a garishly expensive meal and filled up the dinner conversation with a stream of overly rehearsed pro-porno speak. Everything she said was calculated to impress us, though she had misjudged her audience. Not that I wasn't trying to be open-minded, but the arguments she used to justify her lifestyle had little resonance for me. Great, I thought, you make a lot of money, drive an expensive car, and live in a big empty condo. Big deal!

The next day, she announced that she was taking us to a porno set in the suburbs to "meet everybody" and see how normal the business really was. I panicked. She told me not to worry, and that O. J. Simpson had recently visited a similar set and had a great time. I couldn't tell what was more ridiculous: going to a porno set or being compared to O. J. Simpson.

The setting for the film was a large, nondescript tract house just outside of the city that had been rented for the day. The model of so-called normalcy upheld by the form and image of the house seemed to explain something about our society's need for pornography. Like most suburban houses, it was contrived to accommodate a routine of predigested behaviors; it felt like a stage-set for the perfect family sitcom. It was obvious why such a house made an excellent location for a porno film: its rigid, antiseptic, and alienating conservatism practically cried out for raunchy sexual abandon as compensation for the repressed and frigid ideological plots that it harbored.

The house seemed to exude loneliness and sexual frustration all the way down to its foundation. The filmmakers understood this perfectly and responded with an uncanny sensitivity for mining the repressed subtext of each of the interior settings. The stairway, the kitchen table, the chopping blocks in the kitchen, and the basement exercise room all produced their own debauched sexual deconstructions.

As filming began we witnessed multiple couples grinding away in the master bedroom, anal penetration against the kitchen counter, and an all-out orgy on the rear deck. Wedding pictures hung on the wall were rattled by the banging thrusts of hips rammed against them. Overstuffed dolls and pillows were plowed away to accommodate the piling of sweaty bodies upon floral-pattern sheets and decorative carpets. Tossed into a garbled heap and fornicated upon could be found all the standardized trophies of family pride and contentment.

In contrast to the on-camera action, the members of the crew couldn't have been more unremarkable. If the camera recorded licentious, forbidden, and unabashed sex, the lives of those behind them were completely the opposite. They were hardly the big seedy guys with slick black hair and sunglasses that I had expected. They looked more like overgrown

adolescents from the mall video arcade: frumpy posture, stomachs sticking out beneath t-shirts turned inside-out, long shorts, and leather high-tops with mismatched socks.

If exhibitionism and the desire for a particular type of sexual promiscuity are the backlash of the failed promises of suburbia, then these guys were symptomatic of an even more advanced state in which subjects are effectively neutered by their surroundings. There isn't any moral or ethical orientation to challenge, shock, or offend because they have none. To them, there is little difference between playing video games, eating pizza, and stepping over a group of naked humans humping on the kitchen floor. They could be watering the lawn or filming a porno movie—it made absolutely no difference to them.

This became even clearer when the actors themselves hung out with the crew between takes and during breaks. They would all sit around drinking Cokes and talking in the most normal way you could imagine, completely blasé and indifferent to the fact that some of them were completely naked and had just been seen screwing to the point of exhaustion a moment before.

After an hour or so, we got used to the strangeness of the setting, and boredom set in. Although Heather pretended to want us to see how "normal" and cool everybody was, she was disappointed by how quickly we lost interest. For her, the attraction stemmed from the paradoxical sense that she was doing something rebellious and forbidden while simultaneously achieving material comfort and security. She wanted to be conventionally successful while acting out in unconventional ways.

Once the stigma of outrageous sex faded, her job appeared to us mechanical and banal, and the environment boring. Any sordidness with which the films may have been charged had more to do with the particular psychosexual filters though which they would be consumed than anything happening on screen. The methods and narratives with which the familiar domestic settings were infused with raunchiness quickly became as predictable and mundane as the backdrops against which they appeared.

The next chapter of Heather's life was as depressing as the films she made. Through her career as a highly publicized porn star, she encountered many celebrities and eventually fell in love with a major-league baseball player. The baseball player asked her to marry him, with the condition that she quit the porno business. It seemed the part of her life that had initially appealed to his fantasy had come to play a different role in his imagination of her as his wife. Heather agreed to the conditions of his proposal; a wedding date was set.

Before the wedding her fiancé informed his family about Heather's background in pornography. His mother was offended, hysterical, and forbade her son from marrying Heather. He realized that their life together would always suffer from people's negative image of her. He eventually abandoned her, too. Heather was heartbroken and, unable to recover from the blow, slipped back into drug addiction.

We all lost track of her, except for an occasional rumor about her downward spiral into increasingly desperate circumstances. The last I heard, she had been arrested for involuntary manslaughter. It seems she had handcuffed a sexual partner to a hotel-room bed and then accidentally set fire to the mattress with a cigarette. She went running to find a fire extinguisher but got lost and couldn't remember the room number until it was too late.

08

Real

When I was seventeen…

...I was anxious to go out and see the world. I despised the suburbs where I grew up but had never lived anywhere else. I must have been weighing heavily upon my father's nerves, too, because when I mentioned that I wanted to finish high school early and travel to North Africa, he was uncharacteristically encouraging, if somewhat incredulous.

He was ready for me to leave home, but he was dubious about the trip. He asked me how I expected to pay for it, as though he was certain that I didn't have any money, and told me that it was time to start dealing with the "real" world and get a job. In a sudden moment of panic at the prospect of having to work, I told him I had a plan to raise the travel money and that as soon as I had collected $3,000 I would be on my way.

He laughed in my face and asked what kind of plan I was talking about. I told him that I would be taking the casino bus from Philadelphia to Atlantic City where I planned to successfully convert my $40 savings into the needed travel money at the roulette wheel. He laughed even harder and told me with egregious sarcasm that, were I able to pull off such a miracle, he would happily drive me to the airport himself. Otherwise, I'd better get my act together.

I was angered by his predictable lack of confidence in me and determined to prove him wrong. I looked up the schedule for Bally's Casino bus and planned accordingly. I was underage, so I put on the sports jacket I wore to weddings and funerals and tried to appear older. I'm sure I didn't fool anybody, but I did manage to shoot past the ID checkers at the entrance and, after getting $40s' worth of chips from the cashier, headed to the roulette wheels. I promised myself that I would keep gambling until I reached $3,000 and quit the moment I did.

Things started off poorly as I lost the first few bets, but then they picked up. When I reached the $2,000 mark I panicked, telling myself that I could still manage to travel somewhere good for less than $3,000. Something inside me bridled at my cowardice and forced me to continue. After a few more bets I hit my mark and cashed out—mission accomplished.

Back home, I locked myself in my bedroom and counted out $100 bills on my bed. I had expected to enjoy proving my father wrong, but now I was afraid he would thwart my plans for some other reason. I approached him cautiously in the living room and asked if he remembered what he had said about giving me permission to travel if I raised the money. He said "Yeah" in a mocking tone, and asked me when I was planning to head down to the casinos. I told him that I had just returned and showed him the cash. He stared at it with utter befuddlement that quickly turned into anger: he didn't believe me.

He thought I must have been dealing drugs or stealing or something else possibly illegal and definitely bad. He kept saying that a person doesn't just walk into a casino and win $3,000 for a trip. Eventually he had no choice but to believe me, as I was neither a drug dealer nor a thief nor that good a liar. He told me that he was disappointed that this "fantasy" had accidentally played out in my favor, because it was going to distort my sense of how things really worked and it would make it difficult for me in the future when, confronted with real demands, my fantasies would have no solution.

I made plans to go to Egypt: the pyramids, Karnak, Luxor, and Queen Hatshepsut's temple. I knew nothing about these places other than what I had seen in photographs. They were as unreal to me as the picture of the pyramids on my new money. In fact, they were more unreal to me than any place I had ever been, which is why I couldn't wait to visit them in person.

When my flight landed in Cairo, I was overwhelmed with fear and excitement. I had no idea where I was and couldn't understand a word of Arabic or French. The world felt like it was spinning out of control, and there was nothing I could do to stop it. Everything was fresh, vivid, and open to new interpretations; I loved it. That I was able to function in this mode for as long as I did is a feat that I will never comprehend.

Given the precariousness of my situation, I should have been abducted, knifed, or murdered, but I wasn't; no food poisoning, no starvation, absolutely nothing bad—at least not right away. I began my travels with a journey deep into the Sahara Desert—an eleven-hour bus ride to what felt like the edge of the universe. I had thought I would cleanse my visual palette with vast open space in preparation for the pyramids.

I spent a week drifting from one featureless destination to another in anticipation of the upcoming trip to Cheops. I fantasized that I was on an epic journey of self-discovery and that the ancient Egyptian architecture would teach me something amazing about the world and my place in it. I was almost certain that the pyramids would transform me from the person I was into someone better.

By the time I arrived in Giza, I was so confused that I couldn't tell what was real and what was not. I hadn't encountered another

English speaker in over two weeks, and I was beginning to experience the conversations inside my head as if they were with actual people. I talked to myself constantly and performed my own internal reality checks. "Am I crazy?" I would regularly ask myself, to which the invariable reply was "No." I was surrounded by masses of people yet felt alone, as if I were producing scenery out of my imagination and populating it with an army of film-set extras.

I felt like my sense of self was giving way to the voice of a radio sports commentator narrating my decline from the outside: "Right now he's confusing fiction for fact, but soon everything will be back to normal." I was worried: the inner commentary was incessant and I rationalized like crazy just to stay in touch with reality. I made reports to myself about what was happening: "OK, I'm walking to the door and asking this man how to get to the pyramids. I'm buying a bus ticket and appearing normal to everybody around. I'm smiling at the bus driver, but not too much, and walking with a sensible gait. I'll sit down next to that woman over there but not make eye contact with her..."

As our bus pulled into the station at Giza, my heart raced. The area was too congested for me to see where I was. I stepped off the bus into a throng of beggars, salesmen, and guides for hire. It seemed like everyone had been awaiting my arrival and each wanted a piece of me. Legless children tugged at my pant legs and demanded money while sleazy looking young men with forced smiles and new leather jackets competed with one another for my attention. I reported to myself that I was about to walk away but saw myself vomiting in the direction of an outraged beggar instead.

As I fell to the ground, the crowd pressed up against me from every side. I felt my bag and my camera being loosened from my grip. At first I assumed people were trying to help me, but then I realized that I was being robbed. Strange hands rummaged though my pockets and a swarm of loud and crazy voices loomed above me. My commentator reported everything back to me, as if he was standing high above the action while I lay there on the pavement staring off at nothing in particular.

After measureless time, I awoke on a cot in a large room full of people, which I eventually realized was a police station.

I sat up and was handed a cup of water by a short man with a black mustache, a long white lab coat, and an old pair of leather sandals. He said something to me in a language I could not understand. I stood up and staggered toward the door. When I stepped outside, I looked up and unexpectedly saw, right there in front of me, the massive pyramid I had come all this way to experience.

I was already emotionally spent and disoriented, and this startling impression of the pyramid dumbfounded me. The giant wedge loomed over me like an imposter, a fake, a massive piece of airbrushed Styrofoam. It looked more like a castaway from a Disney World seconds sale than the key to life's mysteries. I preferred the image of it printed on my money to the real thing.

I wondered to myself if what I was seeing was the real pyramid or merely a projection, a kind of emergency escape hatch from the bad things that were happening to me. Just then I heard the voice of a woman speaking English with a British accent. Unable to distinguish this particular voice from the many inside my head, I shouted out toward it.

A woman about my age grabbed my hand and helped me to my feet. She introduced herself and told me she was English and that she was going to take care of me. Perhaps it was the sudden joy of being able to understand spoken language for the first time in weeks, or simply the sensation of her hand in mine, but I trusted her completely and was eager to turn my fate over to her.

After rescuing me from the police, she suggested we go for some hot mint tea. This alarmed me, as I had read in my visitor's guide to Egypt that tourists should never drink

•••

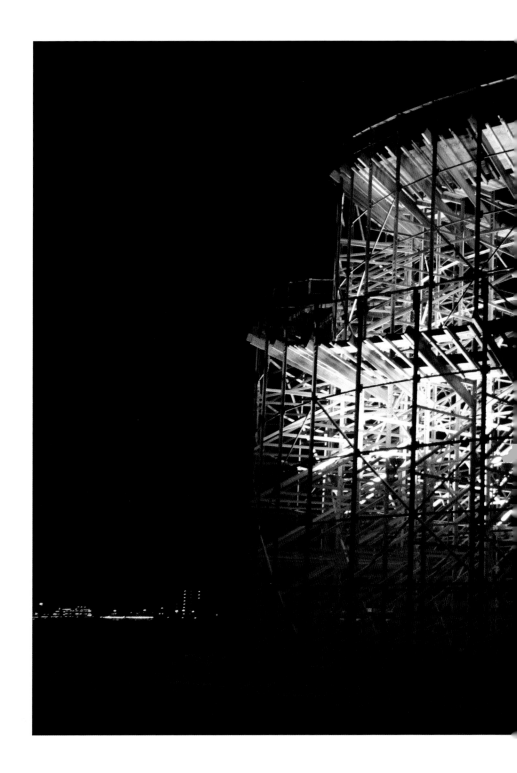

mint tea with strangers because it was a popular means used by Egyptian thieves and drug dealers to drug tourists. I told myself that this nice woman couldn't possibly have any malicious intentions and went along.

At the small bar where she took me we were met by three suspicious-looking fellows—also English—who knew my new companion and who seemed to have been expecting us. They, too, acted friendly—as if they wanted to help me—but were far less convincing than the woman.

We drank many glasses of mint tea, and my glass was always kept full. After a while the conversation stopped, and I began to feel increasingly uncomfortable. The woman and one of the men kept getting up from the table to speak with one another in the far corner of the room. Each time they returned, the woman looked more upset. Apparently they were arguing about something, but I couldn't tell what.

After a while they announced that it was time to go. I was alarmed and unsure of the situation. Watching the woman become increasingly distraught had disturbed me. I didn't know what the problem was, though I guessed that it involved me. I tried to leave, thanking them for their company and saying that I would go off to find a hotel, but they ignored me, and we all crowded into a cab that had been waiting outside. They gave the driver instructions in Arabic and we drove off.

We eventually arrived at the Cairo airport. Right before pulling up to the departure drop off area, the woman and one of the men began yelling at one another. The woman was clearly trying to protect me, though it was unclear from what. The man, visibly angry with her, had the cab pull over suddenly

to the side of the road and pushed the woman out onto the sidewalk. She looked at me with sadness in her eyes and ran away.

At this point I tried to get out of the car myself but was unable to do so, as I was sandwiched between two of the men in the backseat. They acted like everything was fine and once again gave the driver instructions that I could not understand. The cab pulled up into a concealed corner of a nearby parking area, and two of the men turned to face me while the third got out and went around to open the trunk of the cab. By this point I was both terrified and a little delirious. I was having trouble seeing.

As the third man was returning to the front seat of the car with a small backpack, I leaped over the front seat and crawled out of the open door. Stumbling, I pulled myself up, managed to duck away from the arms of the men trying to stop me, and ran toward the crowded terminal. I heard shouting and turned back to see the three men racing toward me. I tripped and fell to the ground just as one of them reached me. As he grabbed my arm, a tiny beat-up car full of Egyptian police swerved up besides us at the edge of the curb. The three men suddenly turned and ran in the opposite direction as one of the police-men spoke to me excitedly.

09

Authentic / part 1 /

For authentic buildings to exist…

...there must also be fakes. But how can there be an inauthentic building given that things exist by virtue of their physicality, which is possessed in equal measure by all things? There are forgeries and copies, but those refer to a different kind of authenticity—one predicated upon the simulation of "original" artifacts rather than aesthetic styles and sensibilities. In architecture the term *authenticity* tends to characterize a certain relationship among specific building traditions and sites, materials, and, ironically, their images.

Building materials, such as stone, are associated with permanence because they are long lasting and relatively difficult to destroy. For this reason they have come to signify stability and timelessness. But the image of permanence is no more enduring than any other sign. A piece of plastic laminate may appear to simulate the wood grain of maple, but it is nevertheless an actual piece of plastic laminate. If the perceived value of such laminate comes from its resemblance to maple, then the physical characteristics of plastic laminate are supplanted by the qualities of maple that are projected upon it.

What may appear natural in one configuration may look stylized in another. A hand-built wooden house may appear authentic when viewed as an extension of a single homogenous environment, but the same building positioned between two austere, white modernist buildings would hold a very different meaning. Contrast among different architectural styles, memes, and tropes goes against the terms by which buildings typically cohere and according to which sensory experience is traditionally inscribed with cultural significance. Such a building would, by definition, appear fragmented and incoherent, like an imposter, simulation, or kitsch.

Authentic / part 2 /

A few years ago I traveled to Spain to visit the work of the Russian architect Victor Sezonovich. His work fascinates me for many reasons, including the fact that it reflects the strange and complex life of Sezonovich himself. The architect immigrated to Spain in the 1960s, after having sabotaged his own career in the former Soviet Union by speaking out publicly against the development of a new city center in the town of Odessa, the design of which he had overseen himself.

Sezonovich experienced a change of heart midway through the project because of the overt propaganda strategies behind its inception that required him to give expression to Soviet ideology in the idiom of a traditional regional architectural style. That a single style was believed to convey the values of the locality while simultaneously upholding Communist principles seemed to be an irreconcilable paradox to Sezonovich. He knew he would never convince the authorities to change their outlook, but he wanted to pronounce the disconnection between their notions of an indigenous style and their requirement that it convey the abstract principles of the political regime without recourse to institutionalized styles.

Sezonovich developed an architectural language that would appear to officials as though he was abiding by their standards while at the same time allowing him the opportunity to covertly ridicule them. Although the intention to subvert the dominant building style while simultaneously appearing to conform to it seemed to be an impossible goal, he was confident of his ability to make a single design that would lend itself to conflicting interpretations.

Sezonovich joined together two heretofore mutually exclusive ways of thinking about architecture: the first took conventional materials and construction practices to be the primary determinants of form, and the second reordered the arrangements by which these materials and construction techniques took on iconographic significance. To accomplish the former, he used new configurations of familiar building materials that ran counter to, but performed as well as, traditional methods. In the latter case, he shuffled the relative positioning and scale of symbolic elements such as walls, windows, and doors.

His early work, consisting of a slew of private homes built for Russian dignitaries and a smattering of small civic projects, such as bathhouses, a public market, and a cemetery, generally includes the arrangements of formidable and over-built walls—arranged perpendicularly to one another—that appear to be solid stone from one side and brick or plaster on the other. The walls of these structures typically extend well beyond the edges of the roofs they appear to hold up, and the voids between discontinuous wall segments are filled in with large sheets of glass. At first glance the buildings have an epic quality to them that is contradicted by the somewhat arbitrary arrangement of spaces one discovers walking through them. Secondary circulation corridors open up to spectacular vistas of the countryside while spaces such as living rooms, reception areas, and monumental entryways look out, as if accidentally, upon the backyards and driveways of the banal surroundings that encase them. In one project a massive stone wall extends on both sides beyond the limits of the enclosed interior it fronts. In the center of a this facade is a giant square void that, while appearing to be the entry to the structure, turns out to be nothing more than a storage area for bicycles, laundry machines, and an occasional car.

Despite the tendency of many to categorize Sezonovich's work as particularly sensitive toward the nature of materials and evocative of indigenous Russian building traditions, it is equally immersed in the representational dynamics of materials and the social codes these image-forms uphold. His architecture oscillates paradoxically between the amplification of sensory effects, as it was valorized within the rhetoric of Soviet realism, and the lampooning of the rustic effects with which they were associated by detailing rough and irregular materials like wood and stone until they looked like kitsch. He got away with it initially, but in the end the buildings were so strange that neither proletariat nor state official could stand them. Soon thereafter, he ran out of work and had to leave the Soviet Republic. It was then that he moved to southern Spain, where he spent the rest of his career building houses for rich people.

I traveled to Spain to see this later work and to look for ways to photograph it that were unlike the way it was documented in the popular Spanish press. The media liked to picture it in the same monumental way: primary frontal views framed to appear as though the buildings stood alone on isolated sites. They bracketed out the tacky neighbors and irregular contexts to make everything appear clean, orderly, and regional in the same way. That his work was heralded to be the authentic Spanish architecture of its time was the final irony, given that the architect and the buildings were anything but indigenous.

In books and magazines, Sezonovich's buildings are generally portrayed in carefully composed black-and-white photos that focus on giant fortifications and mythical entryways. Massive stone driveways curve through landscapes like the processional road to the Parthenon, but in reality the destination is not a temple at the scale of a city but rather a single-family home. Entry stairs are amplified into monumental structures that lead to insignificant destinations. Real entryways are downplayed, whereas garage doors take on the symbolism of the primary gateway. These houses appear safe, secure, and well protected—the obvious desire of their wealthy owners—

but the images of security and isolation are amplified well beyond the requirements for privacy: they are tiny fortresses.

At times the large stone walls give the impression of a paper-thin veneer or wallpaper. One half expects to turn the corner to discover a network of temporary stays rigged to prop up an image of indestructible weightiness that, upon closer inspection, actually flaps in the wind. Sezonovich's walls are like tenuous drapes that barely conceal what is on the other side. On one side they appear massive and monumental; on the other, like a trompe-l'œil mural.

Sezonovich's architecture doesn't seem insincere or duplicitous, just uncertain about reality. The walls have nothing to do: they have no real loads to bear nor civic function to perform. They are overinflated screens, mocking their own lack of economy, purposelessness, and equivocal symbolism. Yet, by keeping the poles of sensorial experience and representation in flux, this architecture counters the conventional rhetoric of literalism and direct experience generally associated with regional and propagandistic architecture. In this sense, he achieved the goals he formulated before leaving the Soviet Union.

10

Blank

My friend Amanda is intensely interested…

...in everything about contemporary art and design. She knows about every artist, publication, or exhibition, follows the news about every art-related event, and reads every review. At any moment she knows more about what is going on in the New York art scene than anybody else in the world. The funny thing is that she lives in a small town in Nebraska, which she hardly ever leaves.

One day she emailed me to let me know that she had decided to build a minimalist art gallery in her hometown. I replied that I was excited for her but surprised because I didn't know there were art buyers in her remote area. She responded that she had a lot of ideas about how it could work and that the site for the building would be, more or less, in the middle of a cornfield.

Amanda's preoccupation with minimalism was revealed by the amount of detail she gave about whatever it was she spoke of: no piece of information was too insignificant to draw out into a lengthy monologue. She seemed afraid of what might happen if the talking stopped, or worse, went in an unforeseeable direction. She slowed everything down until it lost its flavor, like over-masticated meat. She seemed to think that by reducing everything to a single interpretation, or set of meanings, she might do away with interpretation all together.

That was Amanda: a human vacuum perpetually on guard against chaos and disorder. In the middle of a cornfield, a food store, or a cocktail party, she remained the same. Her hyperawareness of her inability to control anything caused her to retreat from everything. She sacrificed her connection with the world for the false sense of security that comes from the categorical avoidance of complexity, conflict, and multiplicity.

She wrote me an email before canceling yet another in an endless succession of cancelled trips.

I almost went to the Judd exhibit at the MoMA last week. At first I wasn't sure if I could go because I had planned to paint the legs of the lawn furniture after I noticed some mold creeping up on them the other day. But I looked at the schedule and realized that with some effort, I could rearrange a few things and actually get to the lawn chairs a day sooner than expected, assuming of course that the preservative I ordered through the hardware store last week arrived on time. If it didn't, I knew I'd have to cancel the trip entirely. Then there was the matter of finding maps, and the most efficient routes for getting from the hotel to the gallery, and deciding where I would have my coffee each morning before the MoMA opened up for the day, and if they didn't have my brand of decaf, I knew I wouldn't be able to sleep well at night and that would ruin my day, every day.

When construction began on the new gallery, it was nightmarish for her. Any deviation from her idea of perfection was traumatic: "Look up there, can you believe it? A hairline fracture in the plaster already!" The contractors kept getting stoned, either to shield themselves from her obsessive tirades or because that was their standard mode of operation. A dip in the sheetrock or a dent in the exterior plaster would send her into tizzy. At each day's end, she was exhausted and on the verge of tears. Some days, when she couldn't handle any more turmoil, she would lie in bed all day and stare at her blank ceiling.

When the gallery was finally finished, she opened it. Amanda preferred not to make any announcements, thinking that the word-of-mouth buzz would add "aura" to the art destination that she had created. Like Beacon or Marfa, she hoped to attract a broad cross section of the world's art pilgrims to her overlooked part of the world. She even followed the tradition of many new museums and considered the first exhibit to be the building itself. She would leave the walls empty and not charge admission—for this one.

Amanda unlocked the doors every morning precisely at 9:00 a.m. and closed them at 4:30 p.m. She sat in the gallery all day, every day, and studied the patterns of light moving through the space. When dust would build up in the corners, she would sweep, and on Mondays, she would squeegee both sides of all of the windows. Amanda contemplated a selection of gray fonts for the new gallery letterhead but put off making a decision.

As time passed the gallery amassed more and more minimal art and, because Amanda never sold anything, the space filled up with stuff. At first she tried to maintain the appearance of emptiness by stuffing things behind walls, in closets and inside the bathroom—like a child cleaning up their room by shoving everything under the bed. But when she ran out of places to hide things, she decided she needed to build additional space.

After many months of hard work, she came up with a suitable solution and constructed three ancillary volumes that extended out from the rear of the existing building. The protrusions were hidden from sight except when viewed from the sides or rear, where they appeared like giant tentacles growing out of the larger white box. Each of the extensions was painted black as if to signify their nonexistence. Inside one felt the force of these overstuffed and denied areas pressing against the pure and pristine empty space, as if about to burst.

One day Amanda arrived in the morning to find a tiny piece of graffiti scribbled on the outside of the building in pencil by the front door. In lower case letters it said: "fuck this." Amanda went absolutely berserk. If minimalist art was about providing a screen against which the myriad features of the world would be projected, then she preferred the blank screen with the projector shut off. An empty screen was better than an imperfect one.

As time passed, the gallery turned into something more like a bunker than a showcase. Amanda kept the drapes closed to keep the UV rays from damaging anything and only allowed visitors by appointment. She retreated into her empty container and kept the world at bay. In the end, a minimized world was easier to manage than minimal art.

11

The Deep End

Script synopsis /

The Deep End is a film within a film, in which the transformation of one life is contrasted by the disintegration of another. Two parallel narratives are intertwined within the structure of this film about the making of a film. The main characters, Casper and Phil, are separated by the logic of the double narrative, until the very end when the two stories intersect and the characters meet.

a. CASPER,

   a young man from the city, has run off into the woods in order to experience the world more directly. He seeks out the "real" in the realm of farm life in the country and regards nature to be the absence of culture, rather than a subset of it. His life is turned around when he accidentally discovers a mysterious phosphorescent substance in the woods that prompts his return to the city.

b. PHIL,

   A movie-set carpenter, is looking for his identity in the things he builds, but his high standards are unappreciated by the film culture, where things are only as good as they look. The greater pressure he feels to make things quickly, the more obsessive about them he becomes. As his sense of control diminishes, he becomes increasingly more preoccupied with inconsequential details, until the very end when his inability to compromise precipitates his final demise.

c. VERONIKA, SUSAN

   Along with Casper and Phil is Veronika, the film's director, and Susan, the producer. Veronika and Susan do not like one another but are required to interact on a regular basis because of their roles in the making of the film.

Character Profiles /
CASPER

As a child Casper was taunted and tortured by the other kids in his Brooklyn neighborhood. Because he was thin, introspective, and shy, he made an easy target for the others—not necessarily for the bullies, for whom he was too pathetic a victim—but for the other relatively meek and skinny kids with glasses, who themselves wanted to elevate their own lowly status by enacting some distinction between their own standing and Casper's.

After a time the daily trauma of living in fear of the other children became so unbearable that Casper was taken out of school, and he spent most of his time at home. He didn't miss the other children—as he had never enjoyed their company—but he felt oppressed by the indoor world into which they had forced him to retreat. He acted out in various ways, by leaving dirty dishes around the house, hiding garbage under his bed, and refusing to bathe. His parents didn't know what to do to help him and were torn between either accepting his strange behavior as his way of coping with things or punishing him for it as a means of forcing him to adjust to the world.

At a certain point, he began to wet his bed on a regular basis. Day after day his mother would come to his room to discover a newly soiled set of sheets on his bed. Casper never said anything about it, but his shame was obvious. Initially, his parents hoped that the bed-wetting would stop if they made fun of him for it, but their jokes only increased his malaise. They figured that Casper's bad behavior would cease if they made him feel ashamed and guilty about it, rather than recognizing that the problems themselves were already the manifestations of those very emotions. Casper's mother yelled at him and accused him of wetting his bed to spite her. When she would do this he would simply sit before her, detached and silent, riveted by the intensity of her emotional outbursts but unable to respond.

One day he looked out of his window to find a large group of neighborhood kids pointing up at him and laughing. Looking toward the side of his house, he saw his stained bed-sheets hanging from the clothesline—a large irregular target of dark yellow centered upon a pure white background. Casper refused to leave his bedroom for years afterward. He stayed there alone, immersed in books about religion, philosophy, and the meaning of life.

PHIL

When Phil was fourteen, he made money by raking leaves for people in the Berkeley neighborhood where he lived. One day he did some work for a man he didn't know but who lived on the same block as he and his family. When he was finished, the man absent-mindedly invited him to wait in the living room while he went to get his wallet in another room. Immediately Phil noticed various things in the room that belonged to his mother. Puzzled, he walked into the bedroom where the man had gone to get money and saw a pair of his mother's shoes in the closet and a photograph of her on the table next to the bed. Without saying a word, Phil left the house and returned home.

He started to notice things about his mother's behavior that he hadn't before and that confirmed his suspicion of her double-life. Phil began a lengthy process of trying to catch his mother in the act of her deception. He constantly asked her where she had been, where she was going, and when she would be back. After a short time, it became obvious to his mother that something was very wrong with Phil, who had become increasingly distant and sad. At her demand he eventually told her what he knew. She responded that it was none of his business and berated him for having violated her privacy.

Shortly thereafter Phil heard his parents arguing with one another on a regular basis. There was increasing resentment and hostility between them and soon the constant fighting gave way to a cold and detached silence. The tension in the house became unbearable for Phil. One day he and his parents were driving across the Bay Bridge from San Francisco to Oakland. As usual everybody was unhappy and nobody was talking. Phil's mother, who was driving, suddenly moved the car over to the right-hand lane and slammed on the breaks. The drivers behind her screeched on their brakes and swerved to avoid hitting them. Phil was terrified.

His mother sat there motionless, staring off into space. Phil watched her as she slowly looked up into the rearview mirror and locked her eyes blankly with his. She took a deep breath and suddenly pushed open the car door. In a flash she leaped out of the car, dodged an oncoming pickup truck, and rushed toward the edge of the bridge. Phil and his father watched her in stunned horror as she leaped, head first, over the side. The last thing Phil saw were the bottoms of her shoes as they disappeared into thin air.

VERONIKA

Veronika is slowly coming to realize that the way she had been raised to think is at odds with her actual experiences. Not only do her preconceptions prove to be increasingly unfounded, she is starting to feel as though she were brought up according to the wrong user's manual. She is confused and angry and looking for the truth about herself. She imagines the world to be the exact opposite of the way it appears to her. If someone acts friendly toward her, she responds with hostility, and vice-versa.

SUSAN

Susan has the personality of someone without any personality. She is as likely to appear sullen as she is happy, in command of a situation as she is helpless. Dressed up she looks worldly and successful and dressed down, like a homeless person. Susan is better at accomplishing goals set out by others than she is at defining them for herself. She feels suspended between an inability to conceive of herself except through the eyes of others and a need to cling to her subjectivity as evidence that she exists. The more malleable her identity, the more like herself she feels.

Excerpted Scenes Synopses and Film Treatment /

C. / 02 INTERIOR / ON-SET (APPEARS TO BE OFF-CAMERA) /

Veronika is arguing with Susan over the production schedule. Susan tells Veronika whatever it is she wants to hear and then goes off and does whatever she wants. Veronika, by contrast, considers her arguments with Susan to be a necessary means to establishing her own authority on the set. Veronika is constantly in Susan's face, thinking that she is dominating the outwardly compliant Susan while, to Susan, Veronika's aggressiveness only reveals how out of control she actually is.

CUE: Underwater shot of a scuba diver exploring the remains of a sunken concrete ship tipped to one side resting on the ocean floor. The diver measures off different parts of the vessel by photographing a tape measurer extended out across various sections. He moves methodically between image-measures until he notices a discrepancy between what he sees and what the camera has recorded. Visibly agitated, he turns his head back and forth between the tiny screen on his camera and the tape measure pressed against the ship's hull.

A. / 05 EXTERIOR / TRAIN STATION / MORNING /

Casper is traveling north, where he has arranged to work on a farm. As the train moves through the city, he contemplates the cabin in the woods in which he will live. He thinks about his tiny bedroom in Brooklyn and his last conversation with his parents early that morning before leaving. They had accused him of running away from the world rather than learning to deal with it, but he couldn't understand why they considered the daily grind of commuter traffic, fast food, and jobs they hated to be more real than growing vegetables, chopping firewood, and raising animals. "Because you're from Brooklyn," his mother had said, "and people who live on farms don't think about them as escape hatches from the city. In fact, they probably don't even think about 'farms' at all, they just live."

CUE: Black-and-white exterior shot. Raining. Crowded train station. Casper appears still and encapsulated from the world. All around him people are moving frantically, competing for seats, and organizing their baggage in overhead racks. Through the window he watches the enormous space of the station collapsed into tiny dots through the lenslike optics of water droplets attached to the surface of the window.

B. / 07 EXTERIOR / STUDIO LOT / MORNING /

Phil is building the set. It is early morning, and three similarly shaped black cabins have been erected before multiple cameras, screens, and backdrops. Phil sits on the edge of the half-completed scenery looking over the drawings. A tool belt around his waist, pencil behind his ear, he studies a set of construction drawings. He surveys the work to be done.

Phil gets up and walks toward three variously placed transitlike cameras set up on tripods facing the cabin fragments. As Phil looks through each of the viewers, he sees pieces of the fragments in isolation from one another and extending beyond the view frame. The fragments appear complete when observed through the viewers. Phil walks back and forth from one viewer to the next, looking through them and then writing down notes in a small black notebook.

Phil signals to the members of his crew waiting on various forklifts, trucks, and gantries. At his command they begin preparations for loading the pieces onto a large flatbed truck parked nearby. As the cabins are hoisted up into the air, those that had been constructed to appear so thoroughly dug into the ground suddenly hang effortlessly in the sky. On the ground, where the cabins had sat, is a rectangle of grass folded over like the pattern left on carpet by a passing vacuum.

Eventually the truck pulls into a large parking lot that has been cordoned off for the day's filming. The fragments are offloaded and positioned to appear on camera as if standing alone in an open field. To the unedited eye, they create a strange image against the unrelated backdrop of store signage, car traffic, and people milling about hoping to see celebrities.

CUE: *The structures are loaded onto large flatbed trucks and driven slowly across town, like a funeral procession.*

C. / 06 INTERIOR / ON-SET (APPEARING TO BE OFF-CAMERA) /

Everybody on the set is exhausted after the previous day's location shooting. Many of them have asked Veronika to intervene on their behalf against Susan's relentless scheduling. Susan acts as though she is receptive to their complaints, smiling and pretending to be affable, but increases their workload rather than reducing it. When the crew becomes even more frantic she pretends that it is out of her power to change the schedule. Veronika is angry to the point of disbelief with Susan. Unable to control herself, she blows up on the set while Susan sits placidly, staring off at nothing in particular.

CUE: *Shot of soundstage. Camera pans across the strange sequencing of rooms that simultaneously describes the uses for which they are individually intended (bathroom, kitchen, den, etc.) but are arranged haphazardly in relation to one another (kitchen between bedroom and bath, etc.). The impossibility of passing directly from one room to the next makes the spaces seem much farther apart than they actually are.*

A scattered herd of sheep is grazing about. Their arrangement is disorderly and random except for a small cluster that is gathering around what appears to be a tiny lump on the ground. The sheep move around it restlessly, as if agitated, but cannot walk away. Unable to see what they are reacting to, Casper aims the tractor toward them and races up the hill to find out.

As he nears the commotion, Casper realizes that the lump is a lamb lying in the center of the patch of loudly braying sheep. He is panicked and unable to stop the tractor, or deal effectively with the swarming herd of hysterical animals. He is visibly shaken, and the tractor continues to lurch forward, out of his control.

Casper finally brings the tractor to a stop and jumps down. He kicks at the dense cluster of frenzied sheep and works his way toward the center of the ring. He pushes lamb after lamb out of his way, only to have them ram back against his legs. Finally he kicks and crawls his way over their backs and gets his first good glimpse of the lamb lying on its side. It is still alive.

To his horror, Casper sees that the lamb is fully conscious and is staring up at him. Something is clearly wrong with it, but he cannot tell what. He reaches down toward the lamb's uppermost leg and pulls it toward him to get a look at its belly. His eyes water, and he feels as though he is choking. He finally gets a look at the underside of the lamb and practically vomits from what he sees and smells.

The lower portion of the lamb's belly is half-eaten away by a brown paste of maggots. A large patch of bloody, raw flesh is revealed at the middle of the paste, outlined by the vibrating perimeter of encroaching soft-bodied legless larvae chewing away at the lamb's core.

Torn for a moment between his inability to act and resentment for having been confronted by a situation for which he has no solution, he stands there at the center of the herd of wailing sheep.

CUE: *Black-and-white exterior shot. Camera pans across wide grassy hillside field (worm's-eye view). It is daybreak, cold and foggy. Camera zooms in for a close-up of the legion and then back out. Camera zooms out from directly overhead. Shot of Casper, looking up at the sky, tears pouring from his eyes; his body inert, frozen.*

B. / 11 EXTERIOR / STUDIO LOT / DAY /

Phil is working on the construction of three identical cabins. In the final film, a single cabin will appear to exist in only one place, but in order to capture the range of camera angles and atmospheres required, it is necessary to film it in different locations simultaneously and then construct continuity among the various shots in post-production editing.

Many of the scenes in which the cabins will appear are to be shot in grainy black-and-white film, intentionally overexposed to exaggerate the material quality of the imagery. Shots of water will be rendered as dark and foreboding pools of viscous, tarlike substances, and bright skies will be eroded into bare white areas of bleak emptiness that, when projected in the theater, will make parts of the screen look as though there's nothing there.

Phil knows that the cabins are to appear on film like blurry inkblots against a dissolute white sky, but he is overbuilding them well beyond the degree that will be picked up on film. Phil believes there is an ethical dimension to construction: "If you are going to do something, you might as well do it right."

Not only does he ignore the pleas and arguments of producers, directors, and other set carpenters to build things more quickly, according to the specific needs of each shot, but the more people complain, the more obsessive he becomes about insignificant details. He brags about the material efficiency of the things he makes while ignoring the inherent wastefulness of the way he builds them relative to the purposes they serve.

For Phil, *goodness* equals *correctness*, which for him means always making things in the same mechanically precise way. In his view the best person is the one most able to make things like a machine. Rather than always trying to simulate the work of machinery, he has recently begun to explore digital fabrication. At first he was able to talk the studios into purchasing expensive CNC routers by telling them that it would ultimately allow them to build things more efficiently and, therefore, more cost effectively. But lately they have just become a means for Phil to be even more over-the-top about what he makes and how he makes it.

In the case of the cabins, this technology has become a means for him to make all of the necessary pieces of vertical board siding irregular in exactly the same way. He drew up countless diagrams and cut-sheets in order to devise a precise method for creating the same irregular effect by turning some segments upside down and flipping others in order to make them look varied.

In the end Phil's cabins required about six times more work than necessary. When confronted by the studio heads about this excess, his only defense was that they were now tooled-up to build hundreds of similarly eccentric cabins at increasingly affordable costs. Disinterested in the prospect of having to make additional cabin-movies solely to justify Phil's argument, they threatened to fire him.

CUE: *Overhead shot from crane. At first the frame includes the entirety of the set, with each of the cabin fragments, and then the camera slowly zooms into a horizontal eye-level shot of one of them. As the camera moves in, the fragment fills up the shot and appears complete, but as it recedes it appears broken, cut-off, and discontinuous with its surroundings.*

C. / 12 INTERIOR / ON-SET (APPEARS TO BE OFF-CAMERA) /

Veronika walks onto the set with a group of upper-management producers to confront Susan's inability to follow her directions. Susan pretends to be happy to see them, apologizes for any misunderstandings, and promises to be more responsive to Veronika in the future. Veronika, unsatisfied by Susan's eagerness to concede, antagonizes her further by calling her a two-faced, psychotic, passive-aggressive liar whose inability to deal with confrontation marks her as a coward. Susan smiles and looks blankly toward the senior producers, as if to say, "See what a lunatic this woman is?"

CUE: *A group of children playing with a soccer ball on a tennis court. Several of them are trying to kick the ball into the net that divides the court while the others pick it up with their hands and toss it from one side to the other. All of them chasing the ball, all of them colliding.*

Walking through the woods, Casper notices an unusual brightness emanating up from beneath the root of a recently fallen tree. He goes to it and scrapes out a small pile of phosphorescent yellow powder. He stares at the golden substance in his hand and discovers the color to be strangely soothing, as if emitting light from the palm of his hand. He carefully gathers as much of the powder as he can carry in a small pouch and rushes back to the cabin. The trace of luminescent dust on Casper's hands leaves glowing trails against the newly darkened sky.

Examining the dust back at the cabin, Casper feels alive. He experiences an intensity that seems to emanate from the powder and his body simultaneously. The color arouses a strangely familiar sensation, as if generated from a familiar-yet-inaccessible part of his being, unknowable but ever present. The world makes sense to him in a way that his mind rejects.

Casper regards the yellow powder as an opportunity to reconnect with the people he has left behind. He believes the powder to have something good to offer others. His personal history makes him ambivalent about approaching them, but he nevertheless feels compelled to do this. Eventually he decides to mail vials of the powder to various people he has known as well as influential and powerful people he has read about in the newspaper.

The police, unsure of the specific nature of the yellow powder yet suspicious of the unmarked boxes addressed to important people, stage a manhunt for the sender. The media takes notice and broadcasts the story internationally. Casper becomes aware of the impact of his mailings when he reads in a newspaper article that he is suspected of mass-mailing poison. Having assumed that the effect of the yellow powder would speak for itself, he is shocked to learn that he is accused of wrongdoing.

He writes a letter to explain his intentions and exonerate himself from blame:

> I am the mailer of the yellow vials. There is nothing to fear—the color is good, a gift of nature. Everyone who looks at or touches it, regardless of who they are, will experience it in the same way, and thus it offers to the world a new foundation for mutual understanding. The special yellow color doesn't care how we come into contact with it, only that we are open to its special influence. The source of its power is beyond our comprehension, yet its rightness will be apparent to all. It's essential value is transcendent and eludes any attempt to name, contain, or make sense of it.

CUE: *Shot of Casper passing in the dark alongside a small pond. As he nears the water, a phantasmagoria of reflected light fills the screen. Like a mirrored hall full of burning candles, the screen radiates with incandescent light, compounded reflections of flickering luminosity. Casper is barely visible among the play of shadows and light that engulfs him.*

A., B., C. / 17–18 / EXTERIOR / HOUSE LOCATION / DAY–NIGHT /

The cast and crew have gathered for a party at Susan's home, a large house built into the side of a mountain. The shape of the house has been formed to block all views but those facing the ocean and large swimming pool with an

...

infinity edge that borders the horizon. Camera equipment is arranged all around the pool, where the activity is centered. Several unused backdrops from previous shots are pushed to one side, including a large photomural of a rustic cabin interior stretched across a portable scaffold and numerous props.

Phil stands alone at the far end of the pool. He is drinking a lot and slowly going nuts, unable to distinguish between reality and fantasy. He can't decide what he thinks about anything and is talking to himself, making others uncomfortable. As the daylight begins to dissolve into darkness, so too does Phil's grasp of reality.

Phil see members of the cast all around: some are actual members of the film crew and others are those with whom he played the role of set carpenter in the film. As everybody is dressed like a member of the crew, he is unable to differentiate one person from another. He cannot tell where the film ends and reality begins. Everything appears to him as a world within another world, without a center.

Leads from the film are chatting with directors and grips, sound guys and makeup people. Actors who portrayed important celebrities in the film suddenly appear less famous than the bigger talents they represented on-screen. Music is playing, and everybody is drinking. The large pool, lit up from the bottom, casts a warm blue glow that beams up into the sky. Occasionally someone dives into the pool, releasing ripples upon the surface of the water that bounce back from the reflective windows as shadows upon the faces of the guests.

Susan and Veronika are standing in front of several discarded backdrops, chatting intensely and privately, as if sharing a secret. They are standing within six inches of one another, yet, because of the images behind them, they appear to be parts of different worlds. Behind Veronika is a large curtain with the hillside image used in the parking lot scene with Phil and the cabins; Susan stands before a large plate-glass window in which the ocean view, just in front of her, is reflected.

Off to the side of the house, just up the hillside above the level of the patio, is set one of the cabins built by Phil for the previous day's filming. Phil looks up, sees the cabin, and walks quickly toward it, stopping to pick up a sledgehammer lying on the ground. As he reaches the structure, he raises the implement high over his head and begins to bash the tiny hut. Everybody turns toward him, startled by the noise of the exploding wooden planks, simultaneously amused and disturbed by the violence.

PHIL:

"Funny how it only takes five seconds to destroy something that took months to build. Why is that? Why do I bother? Nothing lasts, everything is falling apart all around us, and nobody seems to notice."

He begins to rip at pieces of his own clothing between swings of the sledgehammer, as if he is tearing off bits of himself. He turns to face the watching crowd and stands naked before them with a strange expression on his face.

CUE: Music blaring. Lights flashing like strobes. Pulsing beat. World spinning. Phil moves in a jerking syncopation with the rapid beats of the music. Has a far-off and deranged look in his eyes. The actor who plays Casper in the film steps away from the crowd and moves toward Phil. Phil is unsure if the man coming *toward him is a movie character, an actor, or a real person. Casper, concerned for Phil's well-being, tries to comfort him.*

CASPER:

"Calm down Phil. You need to act yourself, to perform a character, rather than always trying to be yourself. As soon as you think you're yourself, you're dead. When I'm Casper, I'm not really him, I'm just pretending, and when I'm not acting a part, I'm pretending to be an actor not acting."

Susan and Veronika, standing off to the side, watch Phil and Casper interact while discussing the movie's plot and analyzing their behavior.

SUSAN:

"It's funny how one character makes movie sets, building images of unreal things made to appear real, while the other looks for 'the real' by trying to boil everything down to irreducible essences. Phil makes actual things that appear to be other than they are while Casper equates his experience of things with their actual characteristics."

VERONIKA:

"It is funny...isn't it...?"

CUE: Shot of a stream of black water passing quickly around either side of a wedge-shaped boulder that both divides the current and is shaped by it.

12

"Dear Mom"

Hi Mom,

*Thanks for your letter and the stories about the trip—sounds like you had a great time. You asked about the movie project I have been working on (*The Deep End*), so I thought I would tell you a little bit about it. I've been somewhat obsessed with childhood memories lately, and I'm trying to understand why I remember some things much more clearly than others. I can't really tell if what I remember is accurate, but it seems to me that* the way *I recollect the past is more important than knowing exactly what happened. My most vivid memories occurred during the summers. I think about the various houses we rented by the beach and the one we built in Oceanside. I recall the sounds, smells, and textures of random things, like the hot sand burning my feet at the beach and the faded NFL sheets on the bunk beds. Mostly I remember feeling carefree and happy, enthralled by the blue sky and the sounds of waves, and at the same time feeling anxious about the future, preoccupied as I was by a foreboding sense that nothing lasts and everybody dies.*

Do you ever think about how memories change? I remember the same events in different ways. Each version feels true, but altogether they don't add up. I've been picturing the places we used to go and trying to remember how they looked. At first I thought my images of these places were more accurate than my memories of what happened there, but then realized that the appearances of the same things changed from one version to the next. My recollections of the past always seem to be shifting, yet somehow I still expect the places in which they occur to stay the same.

In the film we're experimenting with different pairings of storylines and cinematic styles. We're going to choose two or three visual styles and then mix them up from the kinds of narrative-types with which each is typically associated. One of the styles I want to play with is what we're calling the "timeless aesthetic" genre. Imagine a grainy black-and-white movie, with dark shots of dense fog set against a black sky and errant streams of dappled sunlight. You know, the "eternal moment" effect.

Now picture us using this aesthetic to tell stories that have absolutely nothing to do with that visual sensibility. Switch out the expected themes of solitude and despair and replace them with something like the daily activity in a convenience-store parking lot. I imagine a slow progression of apparent inaction, a lone shopping cart moves here and there as the late afternoon light fades into the warm glow of streetlights, and we zoom into the image of a partially eaten Hershey bar discarded on the pavement.

I wonder how our New Jersey summers of mini-golf and Tastee Freezes would look in a timeless aesthetic movie? I imagine the Garden State Parkway running across the frozen Mongolian tundra with exit signs for places like Mount Ararat and the Dead Sea.

Anyway, I've been sifting through various memories and wondering which ones to use. The happiest day of my life occurred when I was about six years old and spent the weekend at Aunt Hanna's house at the shore with Nana and Granddad. Remember? The memory begins on a perfect morning with the three of us having a great time, and ends that same night with me convulsing in tears from intense pain.

I picture myself going down the large front steps of Aunt Hanna's house, Granddad's giant hand in mine, and the two of us walking together along the uneven sidewalk toward the corner drugstore where he used to take me for ice pops. As we are walking I remember recognizing the fire station across the street, where Uncle Mike was married, and thinking about the wedding day (a memory within another memory) when the firemen let us sit in the driver's seat of the big engine, and then all of us kids finished off the half-empty plastic glasses of champagne left on the tables when the adults started dancing. I was happy then, too, though I recall you and Dad having a fight about something and not talking for days.

Back to the story: when Granddad and I reach the drugstore, the light outside is so bright that the inside of the air-conditioned store is dark at first and then settles into a warm glow. I'm little, and everything towers above me. Granddad leads me to the toy section and lets me pick out a new sand pail and shovel for our day at the beach. I'm ecstatic. I select a small blue plastic bucket with a large flower embossed on the side.

*The shovel has an animated duck figure pressed into its bottom
that I will stamp into the sand at the water's edge.*

*We spend the entire day together at the beach and by late
afternoon my skin is severely burnt. Nana and Granddad are
panicked when they see how completely red my body is, and
I feel bad for upsetting them after such a great day together.
Nana spreads cold cream on me, and I scream from the pain.
Later that night I laid awake shivering and vomiting, all the
while thinking about my blue bucket and the cool ocean breeze.*

*So, what does this have to do with architecture and
the film? A lot of people talk about buildings in terms of
the timeless aesthetic. Some associate real and authentic
experiences with particular kinds of materials and forms that
they believe transcend interpretation. They relate certain kinds
of memories and architectural experiences with the quality of
materials and construction (as if one set of sense-stimulants
could be more authentic than another) and believe that too
much interpretation gets in the way of architecture's ability
to have direct impact upon the people who experience it (as
if sensory experience were any less conditioned by personal
and cultural factors than interpretation). These outlooks tend
to regard sensation as being more real than interpretation—
though I'm not sure why, given that sensations may possibly be
even more subjective than thoughts.*

*Remember that Swiss architect I told you about, Peter
Zumthor? In one of his books,* Thinking Architecture, *he
talks about how the best buildings are just "themselves," do*

*not represent anything and carry no messages. In Zumthor's
words, "they are simply there." I don't think my cheap blue
plastic bucket, Speed Racer lunchbox, or Hot Wheels carrying
case would qualify as having that kind of gravity. Does this
mean my experiences are less significant and authentic than
his? Is my sensory data more impoverished than his because
we spent summers in New Jersey listening to Bad Company
and drinking Sprite rather than foraging mushrooms in the
Black Forest?*

    *What I remember about childhood summers are things
like the lime-green popsicles that I ate one after the other
until my mouth froze and those tiny airplanes pulling
banners along the waterfront with advertisements and cryptic
wedding proposals. I remember the cacophony of multiple
AM radio stations we heard at the beach, blaring all kinds of
music and announcements simultaneously. Remember that
radio ad for the Starns grocery store that they used to play
over and over on all of the stations?*

    *Starns has
    Orange juice in cans.
    Starns has
    Big boneless hams.
    Starns has
    Sandwich bags and cornflakes,
    Icing for your cupcakes,
    Hotdogs and hamburgers, too,
    And big red apples for you!*

Did you know that the owner of Starns had twin sons that are well-known photographers, the Starn Twins? I think you would really like their work. The early stuff is interesting because they explore different ways to make photographs look like physical things, which they are. They print images on torn up and wrinkled paper, cut them apart, and then put them back together with masking tape. They break their frames apart too, removing pieces here and there, and play with different ideas about the relationship of images and frames to the places where they are exhibited.

In the opposite way that the Starn Twins amplify the materiality of photographs, a lot of contemporary architects are interested in making buildings look immaterial. They use shiny, smooth exterior materials to make their buildings appear weightless, placeless, and to create the illusion of abstraction. In a way these illusions of immateriality represent blankness. They are symbols of nothing.

The idea that a building would be nothing more than what it is reminds me of the timeless aesthetic I was telling you about before: if we aestheticize things or places in a certain visual style, or sensibility, we can infer a quality of immediacy upon them that they wouldn't otherwise have. It's all just a question of what it signifies, even if it is dressed in the style of absence, immateriality, or meaninglessness.

Speaking of absence, did I tell you I got a letter from Dad the other day? I hadn't heard from him in years, and this letter shows up in my mailbox out of the blue. I was surprised.

It didn't quite sound like him though. Has he changed, or is it me? Not that you would have any idea, but you must wonder about him from time to time, in a "Whatever happened to that guy?" kind of way. Oddly, his note was typed on business letterhead, as if he was trying to make some official pronouncement to me about our nonrelationship. At the end he wrote: "If I do not receive a reply, I will assume that no reconciliation is possible." I wonder if he realizes that the tone of his letter defeats any possibility for the kind of communication he says he wants?

The black and whiteness of his letter reminded me of the yes/no device I used to imagine as a kid. I figured I had three choices: 1. Affect a similar mask of pseudo-professional distance by typing a formal letter on official stationary, as if too busy with my own important life to find a more appropriate form of expression: "Dear Father, I, too, feel similarly unsatisfied by the lack of effective transactions between us of the heartfelt kind..." 2. Come up with another raw, emotive missive of the sort I used to write as a teenager, but never sent: "You Bastard! I can't believe you have the nerve to torture me like this...!" or 3. Not respond at all.

Unsatisfied by the prospect of all three, I ended up sending him a quick and upbeat note written in bad handwriting on a Christmas card, even though he's Jewish, and it was the middle of August! I figured it was better to try to confuse him than to be manipulated by his pseudoreasoning. He probably thought my reply was just as

manipulative and coldhearted, though, for me, it was an
attempt to meet him halfway. In the end my glib response was
probably less generous than his effort. Oh well.

Did I ever tell you about the time I went with him to pick
up some pictures at a one-hour photo place when I was ten or
eleven? He grabbed the envelope from the clerk and quickly
stuffed it into his pocket without letting me see them. He said
that they were boring pictures of some sites he was studying
for a development project, but I knew he was lying. Many
weeks later I would come across the same envelope while
looking for something in a desk drawer in his office. Right
away I knew I was asking for trouble by looking, but I couldn't
help myself. I opened the envelope and was confronted by
something that, in retrospect, I probably already suspected
but had denied to myself: he was cheating on you with
another woman.

I had no idea how to deal with the situation and felt
forced to pretend that I didn't know what I did, just in
order to function. I felt worried and alone, and the stuff
that normally interested me seemed unreal. I held in my
resentment and grew apart from him and, in some sense,
myself. It wasn't until years later that I realized how angry
I had been at him for hurting me, abandoning you, and
destroying my image of our family. I think my inability to
confront and forgive him as a child has made it difficult for
me to respect him as an adult.

Even now it's hard for me to comprehend how I felt back then. I know I must have forced myself not to think about what I knew was going on with you, him, and the other woman. I must have known his actions marked the beginning of the end of our family, but I can't remember ever thinking about it in linear and rational terms. That I remember some of the details of this time so acutely suggests that the traumatic feelings I was trying to repress actually heightened my awareness of other things, though the sense of personal disconnection runs throughout these memories as well.

When people talk about architecture as a conveyor of direct effects and neutral atmospheres, I think about my childhood and the timeless aesthetic. I picture myself acutely aware of my sensory environment yet cut off and in denial, as if the inability to reason through the sources of its intensity was what made it intense. I think if such sensations really lacked any ulterior structure or substance, they wouldn't have had any impact on me. The intensity they bore on me concerned the transference of one set of intellectual and emotional circumstances into the sensory data of another.

This might explain my endless fascination with odd translations of one form of reasoning and experience into the logic of another, like advertisements that tell people that buying a new car will improve their marriage or when people say, "God bless America." I also like contradictory statements that seem like they shouldn't make sense but do: "The more

I eat, the hungrier I get." Or people known to lie constantly but whose definition of truth is so flexible that it allows them to always feel truthful. I especially like instant messaging on the computer with friends while I am also speaking to them on the phone. When we do this, I play the "opposite game" by typing the inverse of the spoken conversation. I say, "Great to hear from you" while typing "Oh no, not YOU again." I've yet to meet anybody who finds this as amusing as I do.

It seems like we have the ability to think in many different ways simultaneously, but we have been conditioned not to do so. When I play the opposite game, it feels as though communication itself is put into question at the very moment it is occurring. I read that the pianist Glenn Gould used to practice playing classical music by blaring loud rock music into his ears at the same time he rehearsed Beethoven, which made perfect sense to me. As a child the composer Charles Ives apparently witnessed the performance of a two-part musical piece, arranged by his father, which triggered his lifelong obsession with musical counterpoint, opposition, and multiplicity. The performance called for dual marching bands to play different pieces while walking toward one another from opposite sides of a hill. As they approach one another at the bottom, the collective sounds collide into a single cacophony.

Architecture is a bit like a confused symphony—it puts different parts together in the same place without necessarily fitting them together. It's both a thing and a representation of

itself. When we talk about the materiality of buildings, we're
referring to its tactile qualities as well as what those qualities
stand for. Talking about architecture in this way is like
describing Strudel (can you believe I'm still thinking about
a childhood pet after all of these years!) in a self-referential
way: "Strudel is just so Strudel; everything about her is just
so like her." It's our perception of her features that define her
for us, and it's only when she ceases to act like herself that we
understand her identity to be independent of who and what
we perceive her to be.

Architecture is frequently called upon to ease, disguise,
or erase the rift between the way we think about things and
the way we experience them. Some buildings have form,
construction, and appearances that are deemed to be honest,
pure, and objective while others, said to embody irregularity
and contradiction, are held to be the opposite. In either case
the equation of visual experience with truth and morality
is simply the dressing up of a belief system in architectural
garments. We ignore architecture's fundamental equivocations
because we want to believe in the brand of realness it
represents, even though its ability to ape our very conception of
reality is its most important and compelling attribute.

Have you ever noticed how photographs of buildings and
places change our actual experience of them? In some ways
we are becoming more and more conditioned to experience
architecture according to a kind of two-dimensional pictorial

logic projected upon three-dimensional things. Blurred zones and blind spots reflect the logic of photographic images more so than the logic—if there is one—of the physical world itself. We use representations to make sense of places and things, and then mistake the structure of these images for that of the things they represent.

More and more it seems to me that, even though I've been trained to make sense of things from one single perspective at a time, the single view point might be drawn back to include multiple views. Like the time I got so mad at Nick that I suddenly understood him better than I ever had before. The two emotions, anger and empathy, were allowed to co-exist rather than cancel one another out. I think this is what the film is about as well: observing the same subject matter simultaneously through conflicted visual sensibilities; providing sensual seduction and at the same time questioning the mechanics of the seduction.

I wonder if it's possible to think about architecture through a multiplicity of privileged viewpoints as well, to watch it hold together at the same time that it falls apart?

So, that's what I've been thinking about, Mom. I'm not sure if we're going to be able to raise all of the money we need to make The Deep End. *If not, I may try to turn it into a book. Who knows? Send me your news when you have a chance.*

Much love,
K.